The Book of
The Bakewell Show

The Book of
The Bakewell Show

The Little Royal

Linda Robbins and Lesley Draper

HALSGROVE

First published in Great Britain in 2003

British Library Cataloguing-in-Publication Data
A CIP record for this title is available from the British Library

ISBN 1 84114 310 0

HALSGROVE

Halsgrove House
Lower Moor Way
Tiverton, Devon EX16 6SS
Tel: 01884 243242
Fax: 01884 243325
email: sales@halsgrove.com
website: www.halsgrove.com

Frontispiece photograph: *The Solid Fuel Advisory Service dray on parade.* (DT)

Printed and bound in Great Britain by Bookcraft Ltd, Midsomer Norton

Foreword

It is a great pleasure for me to write these few words as an introduction to *The Book of The Bakewell Show: The Little Royal*, bringing back many happy memories of nearly 60 years. The show, which took place on the Thursday after the August Bank Holiday, was looked forward to with keen anticipation for months before (with one eye on the weather). It was the most important draw of the year for all the neighbourhood, the biggest one-day show in England referred to as The Little Royal, where the champions from its namesake, The Royal Show, often came forward to compete again, so that the best stock in the country could be seen by the local farmers.

The first Bakewell Show which I went to was in 1946. I had bought a Hackney mare from my old friend and neighbour at Ashford, George Daybell, and while petrol was still rationed I drove her into Bakewell and tied her to a convenient lamppost while I did the shopping. This mare was later returned to George, who named her Lady Andrew, and she was champion Hackney at Bakewell for five consecutive years – a shared pleasure with the Daybell family.

The committee has always ensured that there is something to please everyone and with changing tastes over the years that still holds good. It is very satisfying to see the best of any breed, whether it be farm stock, cattle, sheep, goats or horses – from giant Shires to Shetland ponies – dogs or poultry. The event sets standards to strive for, whatever your fancy.

The show has always had a strong horticultural section and the present unprecedented popularity of gardening and all that goes with it is well catered for. Owing to its growing success, in 1980 the show expanded to two days, giving even more people the chance to attend and enjoy the great variety of entertainment it provides, as well as learning about how our land is farmed. For my family and myself Bakewell Show has long been an important summer event. We all wish it well for the future.

Deborah Devonshire, Chatsworth
12 April 2003

The Duchess of Devonshire, then Lady Hartington, presenting her trophy for the Hackney champion to George Daybell, won by Lady Andrew, driven by Dick Midgley for the third consecutive year.

Commentating on the centre-ring programme in the late 1950s.

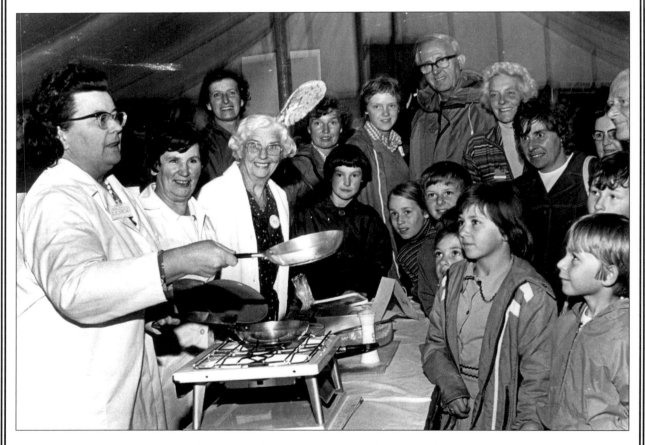

A pancake-tossing demonstration – probably in the WI tent.

Contents

Goat handlers line up for the judges.

Stockman John Archer (right) from Brailsford watches the judging of his Friesian cow. (DET)

Acknowledgements

In compiling this book we gratefully acknowledge the help of: the Directors and Council of Bakewell Agricultural and Horticultural Society, and members past and present who gave their time for interviews and loaned us photographs, the late Lance Waud, without whose initial research we could not have compiled this book, official show photographers Colin Underwood and John McCrindle, Sheffield Newspapers, *Derby Evening Telegraph* and the *Derbyshire Times* for allowing us to reproduce photographs. Acknowledgements are given in brackets after their illustrations.

Thanks also to Bakewell and District Historical Society, George Challenger for resourcing the information regarding the death of an elephant, Derbyshire Local Studies Library and, of course, the many show-goers who have contributed anecdotes and memories.

Farmer Geoff Brailsford shows a young enthusiast how to handle a Friesian. (DT)

Harold MacMillan visited the show in 1960 when he was Prime Minister. He is pictured here with (left to right) the Duchess of Rutland, the Duke of Rutland and the Duchess of Devonshire.

Left: *Early television coverage.*

Below: *An overview of Bakewell Showground in the early 1990s before the Agricultural Centre was built.*

*A class of Dairy Shorthorn in-calf cows at the 1955 show, being judged by Captain
G.O. Archer of Bedfordshire.*

Visitors' admiration for a Middle White sow. (DT)

The Lady Andrew with George Daybell.

The Queen's Red Poll Royal Gloxina (left) lines up with the other cattle in the class. (McC)

❦ One ❦

The Seeds are Sown

Given today's sophisticated organisation, it seems almost inconceivable that Bakewell Show, like many other early agricultural shows, could have started through bar-room boasting. Local farmers gathered in the pub after a long day in the fields and would while away the hours discussing the size of their cabbages, the strength of their bulls, the value of the wool on their sheep. And as the ale flowed the vegetables got bigger, the animals got fatter and the boasts more outrageous until, at closing time, they all agreed to meet again and this time to bring their champion produce/stock with them. Thus the local pub became the focus, not just of a good deal of drinking, but of the very early farming contests.

It is likely, however, that Bakewell Show's founding father, Wootten Burkinshaw Thomas, had less alcoholic and more altruistic reasons for establishing an annual event. A well-known Chesterfield lawyer, Wootten Thomas was concerned about the desperately depressed state of British farming after the long and hugely expensive Napoleonic Wars. The price of farm produce had dropped dramatically and Wootten Thomas wanted to explore ways of helping the poor, struggling farmers.

One way to protect the British farmer was for Parliament to tax imported produce – an idea endorsed by the growing number of agricultural societies being set up all over the country. So it was that on 3 April 1819, Wootten Thomas called a meeting of 12 landowners and farmers at the Angel Inn in Chesterfield. By the end of the meeting it had been decided to form a new agricultural body known as The Scarsdale and High Peak Agricultural Society.

The society would not only join the lobby for legislative protection for British farmers, but would celebrate farming in the north of Derbyshire by holding an annual competition among farmers and breeders who would be invited to exhibit their livestock. Sheffield land agent, valuer and corn inspector Paul Bright was appointed joint secretary/treasurer and the Duke of Devonshire readily agreed to become the new society's first patron. The Duke of Rutland and other landed gentry also enthusiastically supported the new venture.

It was decided that the annual show should alternate between the field next to the Angel Inn, Chesterfield, and the yard and grounds of the Rutland Arms at Bakewell. It is some measure of the drive and enthusiasm of the day that the first show was organised in less than three months. Today the organisation of Bakewell Show is a year-round affair, with contracts for such items as catering and marquee hire negotiated up to three years ahead.

Admittedly the first show was small. There were just 18 classes for horses, cattle, sheep and pigs – and one for the most industrious farm labourer 'who had not applied for parochial relief during the previous year.' Unlike today where there are classes for specific breeds such as Simmental, Limousin, Holstein and Belgian Blue, the first catalogue simply listed short-horned and long-horned cattle. There were no Derbyshire Gritstone, Jacob or Texel sheep, just long-woolled or short-woolled. And of course there were pigs – large breed and small breed – which probably meant Yorkshire Whites and Middle Whites. Sadly there are no longer pigs at Bakewell Show. In 1974 they were dropped from the schedule. This was partly due to regular outbreaks of swine fever, but mainly it reflected the changes in pig breeding. Small units with old-fashioned breeds such as Gloucester Old Spot, Wessex Saddleback and Essex were no longer viable as the large commercial units took over.

That first show on 5 July 1819 was a great success attracting a lot of public interest. When it was over, 60 members of the new agricultural society repaired to the Angel Inn where the inn's landlord Thomas Evinson and his wife had prepared a celebratory supper.

Bakewell Show, which over the coming decades was to be staged at a variety of different venues, had begun...

Right:
Catalogue for
the 1901 show.

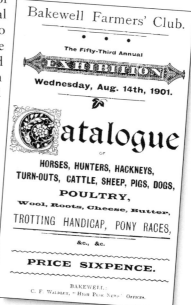

Bakewell Farmers' Club.

• • •

The Fifty-Third Annual

EXHIBITION

Wednesday, Aug. 14th, 1901.

Catalogue

OF

HORSES, HUNTERS, HACKNEYS,
TURN-OUTS, CATTLE, SHEEP, PIGS, DOGS,
POULTRY,
Wool, Roots, Cheese, Butter,
TROTTING HANDICAP, PONY RACES,
&c., &c.

PRICE SIXPENCE.

BAKEWELL:
C. F. WARDLEY, "HIGH PEAK NEWS" OFFICES.

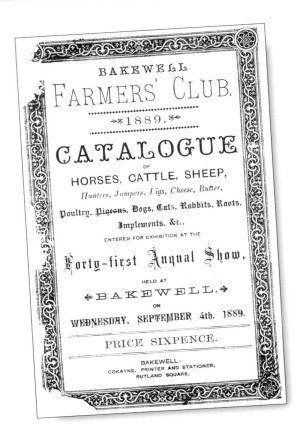

BAKEWELL
FARMERS' CLUB.
1889.
CATALOGUE
OF
HORSES, CATTLE, SHEEP,
Hunters, Jumpers, Pigs, Cheese, Butter,
Poultry, Pigeons, Dogs, Cats, Rabbits, Roots,
Implements, &c.,
ENTERED FOR EXHIBITION AT THE
Forty-first Annual Show,
HELD AT
BAKEWELL,
ON
WEDNESDAY, SEPTEMBER 4th, 1889.
PRICE SIXPENCE.
BAKEWELL:
COKAYNE, PRINTER AND STATIONER,
RUTLAND SQUARE.

'When was the famous Bakewell Pudding really created?' History has always claimed that the cook at the Rutland Arms made her mistake and created the pudding in the 1860s, but in his research show historian Lance Waud discovered that Bakewell Pudding was on the menu at the society's dinners as early as 1843. And in the 1980s that evidence was used in a dispute between two local bakeries, both claiming the right to be known as the 'original'. After his findings were submitted to the solicitors involved, the bakeries agreed to differ and the case did not go to court.

Opposite page: *King Charles II, Wootten Thomas' champion bull at the first show in 1819. The bull, which weighed 22¾ cwts, won the silver cup at Islington for the best bull in the United Kingdom.*

Left: *The front page from the catalogue for the 1889 show.*

Below: *A page from the 1875 catalogue showing the Duke of Devonshire sponsoring the bull class.*

---

447 Ditto : Antwerps, 1y ; these are used for Press News Work, and carry messages
448 Mountney, Large, Bakewell. Antwerps
449 Ditto   ditto   ditto

EXTRA STOCK.
450 Carrington, John N., Bakewell ; Black Carriers

AGRICULTURAL LABOURERS.
Given by the Society.

Class		£	s.	d.
61	To the Farm Labourer, of good character who shall have lived the longest time with a Member of this Society (and having been a Member four years)	1	10	6
	To the Second in merit	1	1	0

William Slater has lived with me and my predecessor, Mr Gregory, 28 years, with a good character.—John Archer, Meadow Place.

James Beechill has lived with us 33 years, with a good character.—L. and G. Furniss, Birchill.

John Holding has lived with me 28 years, and has been a good and faithful servant.—T. W. Gardom, Baslow.

Samuel Slater has lived with me 16 years, with a good character.—William Greaves, Bakewell.

Jonathan Needham has been in my employ 23 years, with a good character.—Joanna Green, Ashford.

Thomas Skidmore has been in my father's employ, the late Henry McConnell, Esq., of Cressbrook, and myself, for 40 years, as a farm labourer, with a good character.—Miss McConnell, Cressbrook.

James Bottom has lived with me 35 years and 6 months with a good character.—George Sheldon, Lowfield.

Benjamin Redfern, has lived with me 18 years, and is an honest, sober, industrious man.—Thomas Swann, Hargate Wall.

| 62 | To the Single Female Farm Servant, above 16 years of age, with a good character, who shall have lived the longest time in the service of a Member of this Society (and having been a Member four years)... | 1 | 10 | 6 |
| | To the Second in merit ... ... | 1 | 1 | 0 |

Hannah Lane has been servant to the late Henry McConnell, Esq., of Cressbrook, and myself, for 13 years, with a good character.—Miss McConnell, Cressbrook.

Maria Buxton has lived with me 7 years and 9 months, with a good character.—Frederick Potter, Harthill Moor.

Charlotte Millicent Gregory, has been in my continued service 9 years, with a good character.—George Taylor, Bakewell.

Successful competitors for the years 1865 to 1873, are not eligible to compete for the premiums in Classes 61 and 62. The successful candidates to be at the Annual General Meeting in January, 1875, to receive their Premiums.

JOHN INGLEBY, PRINTER BY GAS POWER, BAKEWELL.

Catalogue of Entries.

CATTLE.

BULLS.

Given by His Grace the Duke of Devonshire.

Class		£	s.	d.
1	For the best short-horned Bull, two years old and upwards	4	0	0
	Second ditto	2	0	0
	Third ditto *(by the Society)*	1	0	0

1 Archer, John, Meadow Place, roan, 3y 10m

2 Becker, J. L., Fairfield, 2y 7m 2w, *Prince by Prince of the Roses* (29662), by *Cambridge Duke the 4th* (25706), dam, *Princess of Wales*, by *Waverley the 4th* (21084), g.d. *Pomp by Sir John* (12084), g.g.d. *Priscilla,* by *The Bonus* (10922)

3 Crofts, John J., Slitting Mill Farm, 3y 7m, sire *Roseland* (24996), dam *Cherryripe* by *Victor Royal* (30228), g.d. *Cheerful,* by *Swiss Boy* (17072), g.g.d. *Miss Chance by Lord of Braveith* (10465), &c.

4 Crompton, George, Belper, 2y 6m 9d., by *Hind*

5 Hadfield, John, Breck Head, Chinley 2y 6m

6 Potter, Frederick, Harthill Moor, roan, 3y 5m

7 Swatfield, Benjamin, Pilsbury Grange, 2y 4m

Given by the Society.

2	For the best yearling short-horned Bull	4	0	0
	Second ditto	2	0	0
	Third ditto	1	0	0

8 Bark, Henry, Park Farm, Chatsworth, 1y 8m [on sale]

9 Furniss, L. and G., Birchill Farm, 15m, sire, *Gladstone*

10 Hodkin, William, Beeley, roan, 16m, by *Heart of Oak,* dam by *Wellington*

11 Johnson, Robert, Kirk Ireton, 1y 6m

12 Lomas, George, Stodhart Farm, red and white, 1y 6m

13 Wallwin, George, Ashford, roan, 1y 4m

14 Wilton, Thomas, Heathcote, red, 1y 7m

Two

The Show Grows

Wootten Thomas's ideas had clearly caught the imagination of the farming folk of the day, from the aristocracy to the humble herdsman. In the early years membership of the society grew rapidly along with the number of entries for the shows, and to a lesser extent the amount of prize money. Not that that was a concern of the landed gentry who, not wanting to undermine the efforts of less wealthy farmers, entered their stock as 'extras' to be judged but not to qualify for prize money. Their action was magnanimous, but they also had a different agenda. Like the horse-racing fraternity at the time, they held sweepstakes and private matches at a guinea each. The official show judges inspected the animals and placed them in order and the winners took the pool. The owner of the champion bull had to take on an extra duty for his winnings – he had to keep the beast for a year and make it available to service cows belonging to members of the society for a guinea a time.

The Board of Agriculture put its seal of approval on the show in 1821 with the award of a silver vase worth 30 guineas to the best cultivated farm in the society's district. It was won by Wootten Thomas.

By 1827 the society was attracting members from all over the county so it was decided to change its name to Derbyshire Agricultural Society – that year the Peak venue changed too following the building of a new Cattle Market in Bakewell which offered more space than the land by the Rutland Arms.

Traditionally members celebrated the success of the show with a dinner in the evening, when loquacious speeches and toasts went on long into the night. And judging by the menu found by historian Lance Waud, these dinners were not meagre affairs. Various soups were followed by fish – halibut, turbot and cod. Then there was roast, boiled and stewed beef, roast veal, roast pig, roast lamb, roast venison, roast turkeys and geese, boiled mutton, york ham, cold chicken and duck, pigeon pie and calf's-head hash. And if that

wasn't enough, hare, grouse, partridge and pheasant were also served. On the sweet trolley were plum pudding, Bakewell pudding, mince pies, lemon cheesecake, preserve tarts, jelly, custard and blancmange as well as various cheeses – and all for two and sixpence.

The first half of the nineteenth century was a period of tremendous advance in the development of agricultural machinery, and the society, keen to keep members abreast of new developments, wanted it exhibited at the show.

According to Lance Waud, John Spencer of Hopton used the 1832 show to exhibit a new hay- and straw-chopping machine which he had invented. The move proved a big success and he is reported to have sold several on the showground. Two years later Robert Arkwright of Sutton Scarsdale Hall brought a new one-horse tipping cart which he had developed, said to be much more manoeuvrable than its predecessors.

Changing the name to Derbyshire Agricultural Society was fine, but it brought with it organisational problems and in 1835 came a plea from the then vice-president Edmund Chandos-Pole of Radbourne Hall to occasionally hold the show in South Derbyshire, because it was too far for farmers in the south to bring their livestock. Reaction was swift and in 1836 two separate societies were formed – one for North Derbyshire and one for South Derbyshire.

The name may have kept changing, but the landed gentry's enthusiasm for sweepstakes stayed the same. At one point there were as many as 20 side bets to spice up the show for livestock not able to win money in the main competition.

The society was continually on the lookout for new classes to reflect the changes in agriculture, not always with a measure of success. Unfortunately the class for 'the best written statement by a farmer of experiments made with Chilean guana or nitrate of soda or any other introduced manure' in 1837 attracted no entries whatsoever!

Having satisfied the needs of farmers in the south of the county by forming the South Derbyshire Agricultural Society, the spotlight was turned on those living in the east in 1840. William Palmer-Morewood of Alfreton Hall – one of the society's staunchest supporters and president in 1839 – was concerned that because of the 16 miles between Alfreton and Bakewell, few people in the east of the county had ever been to an agricultural show. Most of them didn't have transport, and it was much too far for them and their families to walk there and back in a single day. He successfully convinced the organisers to break with tradition and stage the show at Alfreton Park.

There was another change of venue the following year when the Edensor end of Chatsworth Park was taken over for a massive exhibition of farm machinery – influenced no doubt by that year's president, railway pioneer George Stephenson.

According to Lance Waud the decade of the 1840s was one of the most progressive in British agricultural history. An enormous surge of interest in the industry had seen membership of the Royal Agricultural Society grow to 12,000 with every county in England and Wales represented.

Farmers' clubs and agricultural societies sprang up all over the country following the RASE ethos of linking developments in agricultural science and technology with practical husbandry. The thirst for knowledge was quenched by the setting up of the Royal Agricultural College, the first of its kind in the country and later the world's first agricultural research centre, in Hertfordshire.

The RASE's first secretary James Hudson was a regular and welcome visitor to North Derbyshire, where the trend for establishing agricultural clubs and societies – not to mention ploughing associations, horticultural societies and flower shows – had grown to almost epidemic proportions.

But while North Derbyshire Agricultural Society appeared on the surface to be prospering, there were rumbles of discontent underneath, especially among some of the tenant farmer members. Two in particular, Lawrence and Peter Furniss, believed that the landed gentry had too much influence and not enough attention was paid to their needs. They complained that the president was always chosen from among the gentry and that most of the cash prizes at the shows went to them too (a supposition which was unfounded because, as we know, they entered 'extra' stock and made their money from the sweepstakes they organised). However, there were other issues too. Through their membership of the RASE the brothers could see the great agricultural revolution taking place, but they did not feel part of it. And Lawrence, through his work of helping to organise the 1843 Royal Show in Derby, came into contact with some very forward-thinking farmers and scientists. His dream with Bakewell Farmers' Club was to establish a forum where farmers could meet together, talk about what

was happening and learn of technical progress from scientists and leading farmers. He was also keen to establish a library where the latest information could be found.

In a very brave move, which could have cost the two tenant farmers their livelihoods, the Furniss brothers called a meeting to set up a club. The notices, posted on trees and barn doors and in windows in the areas surrounding their land at Birchill's Farm, near Bakewell and Pilsley, elicited a small but keen response and Lawrence Furniss' dream became a reality in 1843 when Bakewell Farmers' Club was formed. Most of the members kept their dual membership and continued to support North Derbyshire Agricultural Society, but they also embraced the new club with enthusiasm. They met each month at the Rutland Arms to talk about the improvements taking place in agriculture and set up that precious library.

The society carried on without any apparent animosity towards the new club and the Furniss brothers continued to enter their livestock in the show each year. The 1848 show was again held at Edensor where the latest machinery was on show. One happy exhibitor was Mr Crosskill, who in 1841 had a huge success with his clod-crusher, which, he reported, he had managed to sell to Russia. But the star that year was undoubtedly the cake-breaking machine shown by Mr Nicholson which, as reported by the local paper, 'astonished everyone with the ease with which it broke up a slab of the thickest and hardest cotton cake.'

Then, in 1849, the *entente cordiale* was shattered when Bakewell Farmers' Club decided to develop from being a talking shop and stage to a show of its own... much to the society's disapproval. The first three shows were modest to say the least, with most of the entries coming from the Furniss brothers' farms, augmented – as Lance Waud discovered – by a bull from Mr Gould of Pilsbury Grange, one or two cows from his neighbour Mr Swaffield and entries from Mr Jepson of the Edensor Inn, Mr T. Gregory of Meadow Place and Mr Robert Purseglove of Hillcross Farm, Ashford.

By the fourth show, however, the landed gentry had decided to join in and this was to prove something of a turning-point in the show's history. In a bid to rein in what was increasingly perceived as a renegade organisation, it was suggested that along with other small new clubs it should affiliate with the society and concentrate on disseminating new knowledge rather than struggling to put on shows. No one thought this was a good idea. Dissent rumbled on for a couple of years until the society finally gave in to Bakewell Farmers' Club, changed its name to Chesterfield and East Derbyshire Agricultural Society and decided to hold its own show in Chesterfield.

Thus Bakewell Farmers' Club picked up the Bakewell Show baton. By now there were more than 150 members and their dedication and energy had driven it forward. Lawrence Furniss was very much the driving force, first as the club's secretary and later as president. The *History, Gazetteer and Directory of the County of Derby* published a report in 1857 praising their progress:

Bakewell Farmers Club was established in 1843, principally through the joint exertions of Mr Lawrence Furniss, Birchall Farm and Mr Peter Furniss of Pilsley and may now rank amongst the most influential in the kingdom, being liberally supported by the nobility and gentry of the district, who contribute also largely to the prize fund.

The object it has in view is the promotion of agricultural improvement, for which purpose the members meet monthly, for discussing every subject connected with practical agriculture, and annual premiums are given for every description of farming stock, poultry, cheese, root crops, best cultivated farms etc etc. there is also an excellent library attached to the club, supplied with all the best works and periodicals in agriculture, as they issue from the press, thus offering every facility for members for obtaining the best instruction for practically carrying out the various agricultural improvements of the day.

The annual exhibition of stock etc is held at Bakewell in the month of October and all other meetings of the club are held at the Rutland Arms Hotel, Bakewell. At the annual exhibition in 1856, the Silver Cup, presented by Sir Joseph Paxton MP for the best cultivated farm was awarded to Messrs Furniss, Birchill Farm. Mr L Furniss of Birchill Farm is the secretary.

The 1850s saw the club consolidating and the show continue to grow on its new site, the Cattle Market. With the introduction of poultry to the show the birds and the produce classes went under cover, later moving to the lower room in the Town Hall.

The poultry classes embraced some old breeds, including Dorkings, Brahmas and Spanish with the Derbyshire Redcap making its debut a couple of years later.

There was some dissent among the record-breaking 2,000-strong crowd at the 1870 show which was staged on three different sites. The cattle, sheep and pigs were on the Cattle Market as usual, produce poultry and small livestock were in the market hall and horses, hunters and root crops were in the Meadows. A single jumping competition was held for the first time, which consisted of three hurdles set 40 yards apart with a trench dug to represent a ditch midway between each pair of hurdles. Four years later the name changed again from Bakewell Farmers' Club to Bakewell Agricultural Society.

Dogs made their debut in the 1878 show, attracting 130 entries of which 26 were shepherd dogs and 33 fox terriers – a marked contrast with today's Open Dog Show which sees more than 90 different breeds coming to Bakewell from all over the country.

The following year the entire show decamped to a new site, a 24-acre piece of land known as the Meadows on Belper Road, later to become the Recreation Ground. The date was also moved with the show being held in mid-September, two weeks earlier than usual, resulting in record numbers. It was a particular success for the poultry exhibition – records show a tremendous entry of Old English Game. Rabbits and geese were also on show for the first time. But the crest on which the show was riding in the late 1870s was to come crashing down in the early 1880s. With foot and mouth rampant in the country, livestock entries in 1881 and 1882 were decimated. An unprecedented decision was taken to cancel the 1883 show. When it resumed again in 1884, entries were still down but quality, thankfully, was up.

In a bid to try to attract more entries, organisers decided to change the date again and in 1885 held the show on the first Thursday in September – the idea might have worked had the weather not intervened, with heavy showers keeping visitors away.

The 1890s was a period of growth and consolidation for the society, which prospered on the back of the popularity for Shire horses. The success of the Shire Horse Society with its high-quality shows in London was reflected not just in Bakewell, but in similar shows all over the country. According to Lance Waud North Derbyshire honours went to Joseph Wright of Great Rocks Farm, Tunstead. He twice won the supreme championship at the London show with the celebrated stallion Bury Victor Chief. Other names coming to the fore then were Mr C. Etches of Royston Grange whose grandson and great-grandson were still showing at Bakewell in the late 1980s, the Grimes family of Palterton and Scarcliffe, Lees of Buxton and Widdowson of Inkersall.

As the 1890s drew to a close the society geared itself up to face the challenges of the twentieth century. William Smith, secretary for 27 years, handed over to a Mr J.S. Anthony of Field Farm, Ashford Road, Bakewell, and the committee structure was changed into elected and non-elected members, with elected members appointed on a three-year retiring basis. And as for the show itself, it was agreed to include a horticultural exhibition for the first time... much to the irritation of some of the farming members. This move came about because Bakewell Horticultural and Industrial Society, in dire financial straits, had approached the Agricultural Society with a view to a merger. The number of flower shows and horticultural events in the area had reached saturation point – they felt a merger was their only hope of survival. Many of the farmers objected, but after long and heated discussions it was decided that for a one-year trial they could hold a horticultural exhibition. Today, more than a century later, the horticultural marquee has established itself as an important part of Bakewell Show – the trial was clearly a success.

Sir Roland Burke, president for the third time in 1955, walking the showground with show director Peter Clive.

Far left: *The Tenth Duke of Devonshire, president in 1921 and 1949.*

Left: *The Rt Hon. Charles Waterhouse MP, president in 1920, 1948 and 1966.*

❧ Three ❧

The Twentieth Century Dawns

It was not so much the show as the Shire horse which occupied the society in the early years of the twentieth century. The breeding of Shire horses had become extremely popular and the society felt it had a responsibility to try to help improve the quality of Shire horses in the north of Derbyshire – as many farmers' clubs had done elsewhere in the country.

The subject had been discussed at great length many times before with no conclusion, but when a new secretary took over – William Clark of Alport – it was decided to try to resolve it once and for all. According to Lance Waud, a meeting was held on 14 December 1903 when it was agreed that committee members would go around collecting subscriptions to set up a Shire Horse Fund to finance the hiring of a quality stallion. It was obviously a popular cause; by Easter 1904 the fund had accumulated enough to pay the £80 fee to hire Brandmark – a 16.2 hands five-year-old bay stallion – from John Whitehead's stud at Markeaton Park in Derby. The horse was paraded at the Bakewell Easter Fair before going off to do his duty. By the end of the season almost all of the mares covered were in foal – and there was just £2.14s.8d. left in the fund.

The following year it was the turn of Pearl King from Jos Wainwright's Great Rocks Stud at Wormhill. By 1906 it was agreed that rather than a sub-committee visiting all of the local studs and selecting the hire stallion, the society would invite several well-known breeders to parade their stallions at the Recreation Ground in Bakewell. Whether or not this sounded the death-knell of the scheme is not recorded, but by January 1907 the experiment had been abandoned through lack of funds. It did live on, however, in the Bakewell Shire Foal Challenge Cup – a silver challenge trophy bought for ten guineas by ten members of the society.

But while this was going on the society faced more pressing problems than the Shire horse experiment; the show's very survival had been threatened by another rain-soaked day in 1904 which left it with debts of £300 and little or no reserves. The president, the Duke of Devonshire, launched a disaster fund on the ground which raised £180 and that, together with an overdraft for £100 (for which the committee stood guarantor), helped save the day. But the rising cost of staging the show and the need to

increase prize money meant that the situation clearly could not continue.

Tropical weather in 1906 helped boost attendance – together with the appearance of a number of Shire horses and cattle which had won at the Royal Show, staged that year for the third time in its history at Derby. But catastrophe was to follow in 1907 when pouring rain resulted in the worst attendance for years – and a £200 deficit. Finances were not the only thing to collapse. Overstrain and anxiety caused secretary William Clark to pass out, but happily he was revived by the show's Dr Fentem and allowed to go home.

Traditionally the annual dinner was held on the evening of the show and society stalwarts and the landed gentry would express their views on agricultural affairs. George Stephenson had made powerful speeches in the previous century and the Dukes of Devonshire and Rutland often used the occasion to make political points regarding new legislation. But in a break with tradition in 1908 the long toasts and eloquent speeches were abandoned to save time. The move did not meet with universal approval, as the press recorded: 'it hardly seemed like Bakewell Show to find none of the leading gentlemen of the county expressing their views on agricultural affairs.'

That year's show also saw the re-introduction of the dogs and the poultry, which for some reason had failed to appear in the previous couple of years. There was also an interesting development in the horse classes, and what would appear to be a subtle Government bid to equip its mounted infantry with some 'deep, short-legged, good barrelled cobs of substance.' According to Lance Waud, the Secretary of State for War gave two prizes for a new class of riding horse 'most suitable for mounted infantry

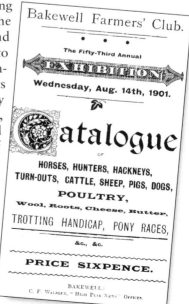

19

purposes', provided that the animals on show were offered for sale to the Army afterwards. This was a shrewd move, but the farmers didn't bite and there were only eight entries in the classes because the farmers knew they could get a better price on the open market than the £30 the Army was offering.

It was crisis time again in 1909 when, despite the rescue plan put in place five years earlier, the society's bank balance had slipped to below £50. They were anxious weeks. For the second time in the new century the show faced possible closure and there were even committee murmurings that the society should be wound up. But the farmers rallied, many of them returning their prize money to the society, and the Dukes of Devonshire and Rutland came up with a rescue plan which would hopefully secure the future of Bakewell Show. They agreed to make good any deficits in the foreseeable future. They had to dig deep for, over the next five years, with the exception of 1913, the gate money and programme receipts failed to cover the cost of prize money and expenses.

There was a crisis of a different kind in 1914. The date for the show had been fixed for 5 August, but as war loomed in Europe no one was really sure if it would take place. Long discussions ensued and the decision was made to go ahead just two weeks beforehand.

Even then the society was not sure if it was the right decision. The Government cancelled all excursion trains – the main way in which spectators were brought to the show – and horseboxes and cattle trucks were commandeered, the Army requisitioned riding horses and the War Agricultural Committee took surplus work horses to form plough teams in grassland areas. Farmers were facing the wholesale call-up of their workforce and as they battled to get the harvest in before the men went, attending the show was probably the last thing on their minds. But the event went ahead and some exhibitors managed to walk their stock to the showground.

Understandably the war put the society's activities and the show on hold – food shortages, the wholesale slaughter of many of the young farm workers in the trenches, and all the other anxieties left little time for the development of farming.

By the time the event had resumed again in 1920, secretary William Clark had gone to set up his own business, Clark's United Breeders, which promoted a new breed called Blue Albion. He had also become involved in reviving the Derbyshire Gritstone Sheep Society. His post was filled by Joseph Wall of Tinkersley Farm, Rowsley.

The first postwar show was held on 11 August on the Meadows. Captain Charles Waterhouse of Middleton Hall was president and it was a jubilant occasion as the countryside celebrated peacetime. Organisers brought back 'trotting' and 'galloway' racing and introduced what was to be a very popular feature – mounted musical chairs. In a bid to involve the younger generation they invited local schoolchildren to enter an essay competition with Bakewell Show as its subject.

The following year, for reasons not recorded, the show was switched from its usual Wednesday to a Saturday, which did not prove to be a good move. Despite being held during a glorious summer and sharing the kudos of the Royal Show being staged in Derby again, there were fewer entries and fewer visitors. The main problem was a clash with several other local events including the Midland Agricultural Society's Show at Alfreton. However, the day was a success for Mr J.E. Mycock of Town Head Farm, Flagg, whose Dairy Shorthorn bull, Airman, won first prize in the newly-introduced premium bull class. According to Lance Waud, the class was a result of The Ministry of Agriculture and Fisheries Livestock Improvement Scheme, designed to give premiums to farmers keeping high-class graded bulls. Another attraction which caught the public imagination was a series of demonstrations by the County Council's Agricultural Education Department. The area was thronged with people watching staff testing milk, making butter and cheese, bottling fruit and illustrating the various aspects of bee-keeping.

Bakewell Show was growing all the time and by 1925 the society was looking for a larger site on which to stage it. Land known as Twenty Acres adjacent to Coombes Road was targeted and show director Roland Burke and committee member Mr C.H. Wright began negotiations. In the end the society agreed to pay the tenant, Bakewell butcher Charles Critchlow, £15, and preparations began to move the show to its new site in 1926. It proved an overwhelming success with more than 20,000 visitors – six times as many as the first postwar show – the weather was perfect and there were lots of new attractions to take the visitors' minds off the fact that the year's General Strike had made money tight.

The Besses o'th'Barn Silver Prize Band from Whitfield in Lancashire entertained, a new shoeing competition attracted a host of local farriers and there was whippet racing. The band and the whippets were Roland Burke's inspired ideas. As Lance Waud writes:

In the 1920s almost every colliery village had its prize band and every miner's home its whippet or lurcher. Roland Burke knew this and drew on the deep-seated affection which mining families have for this aspect of their lives.

The 1926 show was outstanding for another reason – British Friesian cattle were on view for the first time, including beasts from three of Derbyshire's pioneer Friesian breeders. One of them, Frank Gilbert, was particularly noteworthy; he had been to Holland on two official Friesian-buying missions and was later to become the first Derbyshire man to be president of the British Friesian Cattle Society.

Just weeks after the show the committee met and decided to invest £600 of surplus funds – an enormous sum in those days – in five per cent War Stock. The show was again a financial success and the Dukes of Rutland and Devonshire must have breathed a huge sigh of relief.

A decision to drop Blue Albion cattle from the 1927 show schedule because of falling numbers was not popular with the Blue Albion Cattle Society. Their strong protest ended with them brokering a deal with the society whereby if the breed was kept in the schedule they would provide the prize money. It was Blue Albions which former society secretary William Clark had embraced with such enthusiasm in the early part of the century and for which he founded the herd book for the Derbyshire breed.

The decision to cut the pig classification to just three breeds – Large White, Middle White and Wessex Saddleback – went unchallenged.

In 1929 the show lost one of its hardest workers, director Roland Burke, agent to the Chatsworth estate (who had accepted the honour of being director to the Royal Show), but not before he had presided over another change – to the name it bears today: Bakewell Agricultural and Horticultural Society. The move was in recognition of the contribution horticulture had made to the show since the turn of the century and pleased the members who pushed for their inclusion against strong farming opposition.

And the society was to go into the 1930s in a healthy financial state. Somehow, despite a depressed economy, it had accumulated a further £1,000 with which to buy more five per cent War Stock. Now on a much firmer financial footing, the society was able to fulfil its role in supporting farming in general and help fund the Bakewell District Agricultural Organiser Mr A.L. Stickland's proposed series of lectures. He wanted to bring a number of national farming and scientific experts to the district to talk to local farmers. But this largesse appears to have been short-lived because in 1932 the society was looking for economies. Society treasurer John Broadbent (who was also manager of Williams Deacons Bank in Bakewell) headed a sub-committee to look at ways of saving money to combat the acute economic depression which was affecting everyone. On their recommendation prize money was cut and there was a huge reduction in the number of free tickets given out. And on Mr Broadbent's advice the £4,000 invested in War Stock, which was diminishing in capital value anyway, was withdrawn and re-invested in Corporate Loan Bonds.

The parsimony did not extend to donations, it appears. When the Royal Agricultural Society of England wrote asking for a contribution towards staging the Royal Show at Derby for the fifth time in 1933, the society sent £120. A suggestion that maybe Bakewell Show should be cancelled that year in deference to the Royal was not acted upon. And when the

Peak Milk Recording Society, which had been financially supported by the society, wrote saying it was setting up a Pig Recording Society and asking for funds, they too were sent a donation – of £10.

Classes in the late 1930s reflected some of the changes in farming. The 1935 Land Fertility Act included an initiative to give subsidies to farmers to encourage the use of lime and basic slag – something which was particularly relevant to the grassland areas of North Derbyshire. In response Mr E.M. Longsdon of Little Longstone offered to sponsor a class for the improvement of pasture land at the 1938 show. Six exhibitors submitted details of the treatment they had given to land over a period of years to be judged by Bakewell Agricultural Organiser Mr H.E. Wells. The winners got prizes totalling £10. The competition clearly caught the imagination, for in the following year the entry doubled.

The formation of Young Farmers' Clubs at Bakewell, Matlock and Hope Valley was also celebrated at the show with the society's sponsorship of calf-rearing classes for club members only. The class, which called for competitors to rear a heifer calf for 12 months and to keep a diary of its progress recording things such as its diet and the cost of feed, was judged by Professor H.G. Robinson, principal of the Midland Agricultural College.

But by 1939, thoughts were again turning to the prospect of war in Europe. Lance Waud records:

The minutes of the meetings of the society's general committee and its various sub-committees make sombre reading as the year progressed. The war clouds were once more gathering in Europe and the government of the day was again making preparations for putting farming onto a war-time footing.

The 1939 show was held, but farmers' minds were much pre-occupied with the legislation and pronouncements then being promulgated by the government.

At a meeting of the general committee on 13 September 1939 – just ten days after the outbreak of war – it agreed to suspend Bakewell Show for the duration of hostilities. The activities of the society were also severely curtailed with only the crop-growing competitions surviving, with official backing. It was felt that as examples of good husbandry these could play their part in the war effort to increase agricultural production. And the society continued to pay out £10 in prize money to encourage the cultivation of allotments – a sum which increased over the years in association with Derbyshire Home Produce Council.

The secretary Jonathan Hill was given an annual £40 retainer and he, together with director Cradock Hartopp from the Chatsworth estate, who would have been president in 1940, looked after the society until peace was declared.

Opposite page: *Springer spaniels line up for the judges.* (DT)

Above: *Director John Smallman presents a trophy in the Shire-horse section.* (DT)

Right: *An egg-packing machine is demonstrated at the show.*

Below: *Jersey heifers in milk line up for the judges at the 1969 show.* (DET)

Bottom: *Magnificent dray horses paraded at the 1961 show.* (DET)

Below: *Horsepower of a different kind – from the pageant of 1970.*

The Postwar Years

The re-establishment of the show after the Second World War gave the society an opportunity to re-think the range of classes, and the cattle section in particular was the subject of radical change. Blue Albion cattle, which had enjoyed a reprieve courtesy of the Blue Albion Cattle Society in 1927, finally bowed out due to a shortage of numbers and new classes were introduced for Jersey and Guernsey cattle.

But it was what was happening on the national stage which had a greater impact. There was a drive by the Ministry of Agriculture to get all cattle fully attested or licensed tuberculin tested and a motion was put forward to the general committee that all cattle at the show should meet this criteria. It was not a popular proposal, and after a long debate it was agreed that the 1947 show should include both attested and non-attested animals, but on different areas of the showground. This was to prove a logistical nightmare, with even the Ministry's divisional vet questioning whether there was adequate isolation between the two. It was inevitable that non-attested animals would be excluded, which is what happened from 1951 onwards.

As the society went into the 1950s it was on a sufficiently sound financial footing to be able to look at the wider agricultural picture – particularly with a view to encouraging young people in the industry. Committee members met members of the county branches of the National Farmers' Union and the Young Farmers' Club and between them set up a fund – initially with £100 – designed to recognise farm and domestic crafts among the under-25s in Derbyshire. At the same time the prize money for the farms competition, introduced immediately after the war, was doubled to encourage more people to take part.

Confidence was high and there was also talk of making Bakewell into a two-day show. It was the first of many such discussions, but in 1950 it was agreed to remain as Britain's leading one-day show.

By 1953 the society's finances were the envy of many other societies in the UK; there was £18,000 in the bank and a further £1,000 in reserve for show-ground improvements and membership was very strong. The following year was a record-breaker with the number of visitors, trade stands, grandstand book-ings, ground space, prize money and society membership all at an all-time high. New competitions were intro-duced, including one organised by Derbyshire Women's Institute for preserves, cookery, dairy and garden produce and for the first time a ten-foot clock known as 'Electric Eve' was used to time the showjumping classes.

Quite what happened in the 1955 show is uncertain, but what was described by the *Derbyshire Times* as 'a signifi-cant blend of old and new with traditional allied with progress – a programme to excite the imagi-nation and arouse enthusiasm' was a financial flop. Despite a glorious summer day and the highest attendance ever recorded (46,779 paying at the gate) the show made only £140 profit!

Cost-cutting measures were put in place for the following year, but this was not the reason why that show will be remembered. It was to be the last show for honorary director Mr P.J.B. Clive, who had been in the post for ten years, and the annual dinner was cancelled in deference to the political situation in Eastern Europe. Instead guests were invited to make a donation to the Hungarian Relief Fund.

Matthew Longson of Great Longstone had taken over as director and spearheaded a bid to enlarge the main showground to provide more space for the show and for parking. Riverside Farm was on the market, so the society bought it, thus acquiring six acres next to the showground and at a later date a further nine acres were acquired bringing the total area of land owned, or leased by, the society to 42 acres.

There was an interesting first in 1959 when the show appointed a working farmer to be president. Harold Warren of Knouchley Farm, Calver, had been a society member for many years and had worked hard on various committees. The move was warmly welcomed by the rest of the farming community and finally exploded the myth that the landed gentry always got the honour. However, Warren's year of office and the success of the show were threatened by a printers' strike in July at the very height of the event's promotional campaign. Drastic measures saw the show being advertised on commercial television for the first time – and two typists and two housewives from Bakewell spent two days typing out 150 pages of text to enable several thousand show programmes to be published. Both efforts seem to have paid off – the show made £2,344, the highest profit ever.

One of the major attractions that year was the British Showjumping Association competition which attracted top showjumpers including Paddy McMahon riding both his horses Sun Cottage and Tim II. The purse for the winners was worth £190, which seemed very generous for the time. Afterwards Paddy competed in the Derbyshire Area International Trial.

In 1960 there was another first when British Prime Minister Harold MacMillan, who happened to be visiting his nephew, the Duke of Devonshire, came to the show. The PM spent five hours on the showground, being taken around by Matthew Longson. Smoking his pipe and with his walking stick crooked over his arm, he chatted amiably to the crowds and showed a great interest in the British Wool Marketing Board stand where he paused to tell other visitors: 'Britain's greatness was based on wool.' And, as the *Derbyshire Times* reported: 'At the goat section he looked at the animals and remarked that his daughter had once kept goats and they made very fine pets.'

Throughout the development of the show the society stayed true to its original remit to devote time and money to encouraging agricultural development and education, and in the early 1960s it looked at the possibility of awarding a travelling scholarship through the Young Farmers' Clubs. Would-be candidates submitted a five-year management plan for operating a mythical 100-acre West Derbyshire farm. The submission included stocking, cropping, capital investment, cash flow and accounts. There was a healthy entry and after interviewing the finalists, David Else from Nunsfield Farm, Dalbury Lees, was chosen as the winner. The society gave him £75 towards the cost of visiting and studying three European farms.

Back on the showground it was time for change. New floodlighting was erected in time for the 1962 show where eight 1,000-watt lights were mounted on 25ft poles and concentrated on the cattle pens. They were installed a couple of days before the show and switched on for the first time on the Tuesday night. The idea was to help cattle exhibitors and herdsmen to move freely in and out of the pens during the night to attend to their stock. A more significant development, for organisers at least, was the building of a permanent office for the show secretary and staff. Until then the society had met at various offices in Bakewell and administration had been carried out at a variety of venues including the NFU offices and the Chatsworth estate. But the show was growing fast, the workload was increasing and permanent, well-equipped premises were desperately needed. Planning

permission took time, but eventually the wooden structure, which is still there today, was erected for the princely sum of £1,718 – which didn't include the electricity, plumbing and other incidentals.

The 1965 show was a world beater. It was held at the same time as the famous 'Ramboree' when 3,600 Scouts from all over the world descended on Chatsworth Park and were welcomed by Chief Scout Charles MacLean. A number of the Scouts came to Bakewell Show and an impressive display of 80 world flags was raised in the centre ring.

That was the year when a nursery was introduced on the showground for visiting children. Matthew Longson had seen the Red Cross successfully operating them at other shows and thought they would be a welcome innovation at Bakewell. The society provided a special marquee with a wooden floor and lots of toys, including a rocking-horse, and children were able to stay there free. Red Cross Commandant Mrs S. Hancock told the *Derbyshire Times* at the time:

The nursery is an excellent idea both for its own sake and for the fact that it provides proper facilities for mothers and babies who used to have to come into the first aid tent where people were being treated for minor mishaps.

The cost of staging the show was increasing all the time and the society was constantly on the lookout for ways of increasing income and cutting costs. A recruitment drive for more members was launched, entry fees went up and companies and individuals were approached to sponsor the society's activities. One money-spinner was allowing the showground to be used for car parking on Monday market days.

The 1967 show saw the revival of trotting races – not seen at the show since before the war – and the abandonment of senior showjumping. Organisers felt that people perhaps wanted a change. The six races started at 5p.m. with bookies posted at the ringside to take bets. Prizes were donated by the cigarette company John Player. The event had all the ingredients to make it a success, but curiously was not. The following year trotting was abandoned and senior showjumping reinstated.

But for organisers there was a more immediate problem. Despite the fact that the 1967 show had been a great success, it ended with a £500 loss, sparking renewed calls for Bakewell to become a two-day show. Once again there was a great deal of discussion which concluded that rather than extend the event to two days the society would change the day from a Thursday to a Saturday in a bid to attract more visitors. This tactic had been tried before without success and the organisers of events on the same day were very unhappy at the prospect – Leek Agricultural Society in particular feared a drop in entries – but the move went ahead anyway. As then secretary Roland Boocock told the *Derbyshire Times*:

With the five day week and staggered holidays we feel more people will be able to come to shows like Bakewell, weather permitting. We feel we stand a good chance of getting more people to the show at the weekend.

Whether it was the clash of dates that made it a disaster (Derby County and Manchester United, then at the top of the First Division, were also playing that day) records don't reveal, but attendance was down and profits were badly hit. Organisers faced losses of £2,000 and an appeal went out to members for financial help. This raised just £630. It had been billed as the show that had everything; there were extra attractions for children including the famous Chitty Chitty Bang Bang 'fantasmagorical machine', there was a stunning display by the Household Cavalry backed by the Blues and Royals, and the reigning Miss World Eva Rueber Staier was there to add a touch of glamour. Roland Boocock was dumbfounded:

It really is something of a mystery from a show point of view. I thought Saturday was very good and we spared no expense to make sure there was something of interest for everyone. Whether it is because we are not established, I don't know.

It was certainly one of the best shows we have had, we have never provided such a variety of interests and I personally am very happy with it. We had a glorious day and everyone who came seemed to enjoy themselves. It is unfair to judge the show on one Saturday.

The fact that entrance fees had gone up and many visitors deemed car-parking charges too high does not seem to have been considered.

Unfortunately organisers had committed to a three-year experiment so the 1971 show went ahead on the first Saturday in August. It was something of a flagship show in that it was chosen as the venue for one of the Area International Showjumping Trials. One of the riders – and indeed the winner of the trial – was Paddy McMahon on Pennwood Forge Mill (affectionately know as Forgie), who appeared at the show in 1959 and was to go on to take national and international honours. Entries were up in the livestock section, special attractions included an It's a Knockout competition and organisers were confident that attendance too would be better. It was; 21,722 visitors came through the gates and the show almost broke even financially, but the situation needed resolving.

A change of direction and style was once again mooted and many felt that a two-day show was the answer, but the committee stuck to its guns and went for a third year on a Saturday – and instantly ran into trouble. The chosen date clashed with the Derby Kingsway Show and the Kennel Club refused to grant a licence for a dog show in Bakewell because the two venues were so close. This meant moving the show to 22 July, which turned out to be a very wet day. Attendance was half that of the previous year and the show lost £6,000. Again the hat went around the members to raise £2,500 to help defray costs.

Bakewell was not the only society to be struggling; Derbyshire Agricultural Society shared many of the same problems, so the two directors got together to see if they could pool resources and cut costs. But short of a total merger, which neither society wanted, it was impractical to try to run the two shows from a central administration, so the idea was dropped.

Other innovations included organising a spring horse show which, despite being quite well supported, turned out not to be the saviour the society needed. It was held in wet weather and succeeded only in churning up the centre ring. The young farmers tried hard, organising a folk festival which brought in £132 and having a flutter on the Lincolnshire handicap which raised a further £635, but the prospect of a two-day show loomed large.

The 1973 show was held under the shadow of the Markham pit disaster in which more than a dozen miners perished. It had reverted to its familiar Thursday slot with the widespread approval of members, exhibitors and tradespeople alike. The only 'casualties' of the alteration were the showjumpers, whose event clashed with the Dublin Horse Show. In a change to the traditional centre-ring entertainment it was decided to stage a 'Hunt Meet of Days Gone By'. Members of the High Peak and Barlow hunts took part with some people arriving by stagecoach and others dressed in costume following on foot. Another innovation was the introduction of Fisherman's Walk, which has proved an enduring addition to the show and is still one of the most popular areas, thanks to the Duke of Rutland allowing use of the river. Whether it was this that brought back the crowds is not recorded, but it was a bumper show with 24,000 visitors, the highest since 1969.

The new children's favourites, the Wombles, were the star attraction the following year, which saw members sporting the distinctive new Bakewell Show ties with a wheatsheaf motif, introduced for the first time. It also saw the event capitalise on the number of eve-of-show visitors. They decided to charge a modest fee to members of the public wanting to have a good look around, a move which attracted 539 people. Obviously the word spread, because in 1975 that number had risen almost fivefold.

Matthew Longson retired after 18 years as director and his assistant John Smallman took over, soon heading up a completely new team with the appointment of Ted Brownhill as secretary to succeed John Davison – and it was Ted who was to lead the show finally into a two-day event. John Davison's tenure ended in triumph. At the 1975 show he promised the biggest event yet with more for visitors to see and a reorganised trade area which encompassed rings one and two as it had in 'the good old days'. This, he said, would allow for more appropriate types of stand (and more of them), such as agricultural machinery. And for the first time Shire horses were to get a crack at the big time with the champion and reserve champion qualifying to compete on an equal basis at the Horse of the Year Show at Wembley. Davison was not wrong – the show was a great success with a near-record 41,000 visitors, the highest for 14 years. The weather was so hot that many of the crowd suffered from heat exhaustion. But the success threw up the age-old question: could it progress as a one-day event, or would it have to become two days to retain its popularity? An editorial in the *Derbyshire Times* crystallised feeling:

The last show was enjoyed by many, many people, but there were many complaints and we believe show officials, whose attitude to innovation is refreshingly receptive will take account of these when the decision is taken next month whether to remain a one day show or go for two days. They must consider if the show is large enough to cater for the huge crowds turning up if the weather is good. Because this year events ran late, the catering couldn't cope and the beer was warm and nasty by teatime.

Spreading the load over two days could be the answer, but would accommodation be available for a two-day event and are showground facilities up to the task?

These and many other questions need going into deeply before any decision is made, but we hope the show chooses the course which will see it enjoy another 124 years – at least – of success.

But still the decision to go for two days was not made.

The 1976 event was a huge financial success with almost £5,500 profit, but there were fears about rising costs. It was reported that in the three years between 1973 and 1976 the cost of labour, materials, stand hire, shedding and canvas had gone from £9,688 to £18,062 – a £3,000-a-year rise. The committee, convinced it could do little about expenditure, looked for ways of increasing income.

There was a further blow in 1977 when VAT was introduced and looked likely to be added to subscriptions and other income received by the society. It meant putting a surcharge on entry to the show and there were fears that this could affect attendance. As it was VAT didn't kick in until 1979, at which point it had become accepted as inevitable.

Increasingly events were being staged on the preview day, even though Bakewell was still officially a one-day show. In 1977 centre-ring entertainment started at two o'clock on the Wednesday with junior hunters and continued with showjumping right through until 8.30p.m. Still, 45,000 visitors flocked to the show on the Thursday. There was a record number of trade stands – everything from a pin to a tractor, according to pre-publicity – and entries had to

be limited to fit everything in, leading Ted Brownhill to comment: 'I believe there is a case for making this a two-day show if we can count on this kind of support.' Dank drizzly weather hit profits in 1978 and, with income from entrance tickets, the grandstand and parking dropping by £6,513, the show barely broke even. The following year the entire dog section moved to the Wednesday and with events starting at 10a.m. instead of 9a.m., 1979 was virtually a dress rehearsal for the official launch of the show as a two-day event in 1980. It cost more to stage, but it paid dividends – 35,861 people paid to come in and the society made a profit of £5,801.

In fact most of the advertising for 1979 made it appear to be that already. There were no centre-ring attractions, but two teams of skydivers, the Marksman and the Western Jean Company, and two bands, Mansfield Coronets Jazz Band and Bakewell Silver Band, kept crowds entertained in between the showjumping and the dog show.

The Prime Minister Harold MacMillan at the 1960 show, with the show secretary Bill Conway. (McC)

Huntsmen from the Victorian era, from the pageant, early 1970s.

Five

The Two-Day Show

It needed meticulous planning, but the move to two days was seamless. The judging was divided between Wednesday and Thursday, the goat section was moved to Wednesday and trade stands operated on both days. There was great enthusiasm for the new venture and by 1980 Bakewell Show had been recognised as important enough to merit television coverage and Radio Sheffield also broadcast from the show. As secretary Ted Brownhill said at the time: 'I always used to say we were top of the second, but we're certainly in the first division now... the scale of our event means it is bettered only by the big royal shows.'

Indeed everything was right... except the weather – appalling conditions were to torpedo any hopes the society had of a triumphant start to the new two-day event. Some 10,000 fewer people attended and the show made a loss of £5,455. Again members and patrons came to the rescue with donations and sponsorship illustrating, as Lance Waud put it: 'the crucial importance of an underlying solid and supportive membership.'

The show faced another threat in 1981, and this time it had nothing to do with the weather. Proposals had been put forward for a Bakewell bypass which would have driven right through the centre of the showground, and put the future of Bakewell Show at risk. Director John Smallman was called to give evidence and lodged the strongest possible objections on behalf of the society, which seems to have gone a long way to having the plans thrown out. Delighted at the news John Smallman told the *Derby Evening Telegraph*:

The rejection of the by-pass scheme should guarantee our show for the next 20 years. The show is guaranteed for as long as I live. I shall fight any renewed threat to put a road through our ground.

The show was held just a week after the marriage of Prince Charles and Lady Diana Spencer and the feel-good factor which the wedding had engendered was still in the hearts of visitors. The sun shone and bumper crowds turned out to enjoy the first dry show for three years. Even the early-morning downpour on the Thursday failed to dampen spirits.

It was the year of the first lady president from the ranks, Mary Daybell. Daughter of Hackney horse specialist George Daybell, Miss Daybell, a retired health visitor, had been involved with the show since 1924. Her unusual contribution to her year of office was to sign up 50 new members, fellow Soroptimists in Buxton.

It was also the International Year of the Disabled and the show did its bit to support the initiative, giving free entry to disabled people and their carers on the Wednesday. They also had a special area alongside the centre ring for them to watch the entertainment, which included a frisbee-throwing demonstration.

There was a complete break from farming tradition in 1982 when the highlight of the entertainment was a fashion extravaganza put on by Debenhams with proceeds going to the South Atlantic Fund. Security was very tight as seven professional models straight from the catwalks of Paris and Milan paraded furs and fashions worth more than £70,000 at a special show. A decision was taken that year to reinstate the annual dinner, which had not been held for a good many years, and 140 members and their partners gathered at the Edensor Institute for what was described as 'a happy evening'.

The 1980s was the decade of the fun run and everyone who had the stamina would take part in sponsored races in towns and villages throughout the country. It was decided to stage a Bakewell Show race called the Calton Chase at the 1983 show. The gruelling 12-mile course was set to start from the centre ring at 6p.m. on the Wednesday and follow a course along the lower slopes of Calton Hill fringing the showground, climbing the steep hillside and disappearing into the woods. There was to be a radio commentary to keep people on the showground in touch with the action and the last lap would see the athletes reappearing to run down the hill and back into the showground to the finishing line. At least that was how organisers had planned it... In reality the event ended in confusion. Originally there were two dozen entrants – all men. Appeals to drum up support from women runners at the last minute proved fruitless, and on the day only 14 men lined up to start the race. Of them only five actually finished the course – the rest either retired or got lost in the Derbyshire hills. Unsurprisingly secretary Ted Brownhill was heard to comment: 'I think we may need a rethink.'

Zycomm two-way radios had been introduced that year to help officials keep in touch with each other on

Top: *Pony Club games in 1990.* (SN)

Above: *Virginia Crane of Worcestershire arrives with two of her goats at the 1990 show.* (SN)

Left: *Geoffrey Roberts, president in 1990, at the opening ceremony with show director John Smallman and his wife and Revd Edmund Urqhart.* (CU)

Below: *Dahlias on display in the horticultural tent.* (SN)

Above: *The Duchess of Devonshire (right) presenting Miss Mary Daybell with a basket of flowers from exhibitors in 1996 to mark her 50 years as a steward in the Hackney section.*

Right: *A fine turnout in the Hackney class at the 1988 show.* (SN)

Below: *Preparing a cow from the Birchcross Herd from Coal Aston for the ring at the 1989 show.* (SN)

Below right: *President of the 1988 show* Willis White *and his wife* Dorothy (centre) *with the director.* (CU)

Left: *Relaxing prior to the judging for this family with their Friesian cattle – Mr and Mrs George Bonsall, their daughter Elizabeth and nephew Sam Hawksworth of Hartington at the 1990 show.* (SN)

Showjumping at the 1986 event. (SN)

the showground. The year 1983 also saw six dry-stone wallers demonstrating their craft for the first time (and in the process building a permanent wall on the showground) and a falconry display, which proved very popular. The falcons were back in 1984 courtesy of Robert Haddon of Burbage, Leicestershire, and there was a display of rare breeds and cattle from Graves Park Animals Farm run by Shirecliffe College in Sheffield, some of which were led by students in the Grand Parade.

A new feature was introduced in 1987 when president Brian Bakel had the official show opening on the Tuesday evening with a short ecumenical service led by the Vicar of Bakewell, the Revd Edmund Urquhart. The service is still held today when officials offer prayers for good weather. It was boom time again in 1989 when the best attendance since 1961 brought a financially successful show, which must have come as a great relief to the society. A wide-ranging programme of improvements had been carried out over the previous two years and this meant a profitable show could be achieved without dipping into the sinking fund. It was British Food and Farming Year and a special committee was set up to celebrate what was originally intended to be just a one-off exhibition. A marquee was erected, a specialist cheese competition launched and food producers invited to exhibit. No one could have envisaged how successful it would be. The committee became permanent and today, 14 years on, the British food and farming marquee is one of the most popular and best-loved exhibits on the showground. And 1989 was a year when an increasing number of young people were involved, leading director John Smallman to comment in his annual report:

I remember feeling a great deal of pleasure in seeing so many young farmers taking part in the Grand Parade. Although we have a wonderful army of enthusiastic and dedicated volunteers to help run our show, we must always encourage the younger generation to take part thereby securing the future of the society. I hope that a combination of youthful enthusiasm and maintaining the character of an agricultural show will result in someone reporting the success of the 260th show.

Unfortunately his jubilation did not extend to the following year when once again the weather caused havoc. But unlike previous years which had been a washout, this was a burn-out. Two of the hottest days in the show's history saw show-goers wilting in the heat, and a number of animals sent home because of conditions. There were 4,000 fewer people through the gate and the show made what John Smallman described as 'a not insignificant loss'.

When the sinking fund had been established 17 years before it was to cover disastrously wet shows – few could have predicted gate receipts being affected because of fear of sunstroke.

Brian Bakel took over as show director in 1991, the same year that the society finally gave in to new technology and introduced a basic computer system. Over the next couple of years the whole of the show's administration from accounting and competition entries to records of patrons, members and trade stands would become computerised leading to greater efficiency and a more professional look. Bakewell was up there with the major players and it was necessary to demonstrate its forward thinking. Indeed, the status which Bakewell had in the show world was demonstrated by a visit from Food Minister David Maclean to answer questions put to him by members of the society, the National Farmers Union and food lobbying groups. It was something of a coup for the show and the questioners pulled no punches in wanting to know about the real state of farming in the UK.

But playing in the 'big league' meant that the society had to investigate other ways of funding the

An overview of the showground, 1983. (SN)

show. Gate receipts and entry fees nowhere near covered the rising cost of tentage and attractions and unpredictable weather meant it was necessary to keep the sinking fund topped up on a regular basis. Sponsors were very generous and the annual sponsorship lunches brought in renewed support, but the committee needed to find 'big league' sponsorship if the show was to continue to be a success.

The 1993 show was a prime example of how the committee needed to stay ahead of the game. The weather was atrocious and the cost of bringing extra straw and shale onto the ground to try to keep the main walkways open, together with the hire of tractors to pull mud-bound vehicles out, was crippling. The sinking fund simply could not sustain unending losses and with the current structure of the society, committee members were liable if losses outstripped funds.

Two historic decisions were taken. Firstly, it was agreed that the society should become incorporated and secondly, a deal was struck with North Derbyshire motor dealers Gordon Lamb to become the official sponsor of Bakewell Show. Incorporation effectively removed any financial liability from committee members who, in the event of a deficit, were liable only for a nominal sum. The sponsorship deal, which began in 1994, brought in a lump sum to help defray the cost of putting on the show and various fringe benefits including a smart new logo and improved signage for a more professional image. The initial package, which coincided with Gordon Lamb's 40th anniversary, was for three years, but now a decade on it is still in place and looks likely to remain so for the foreseeable future.

Despite the weather, 1993 did have its highlights. A new area called the Village Green was unveiled where traditional craftspeople demonstrated their skills. This included a village bandstand with a rolling programme of musical entertainment and areas for visitors to sit and enjoy their picnics – albeit cocooned in waterproofs. And show patrons were rewarded for their support by a smart new enclosure where they could meet, enjoy a meal and entertain their friends.

It was the year when organisers brought bungee jumping – the latest craze to sweep the country – to Bakewell Show... and probably wished they hadn't. The society found itself embroiled in something of a 'bungee war' which had broken out between two rival companies. They both claimed the right to bring the 180ft tower onto the showground and encourage fearless people to jump from it attached only to a thick

A spinning demonstration at the 1988 show. (SN)

rubber rope. Unfortunately the argument ended up in a 'breach of contract' case which cost the society money it could ill-afford. That, together with the legal costs involved in incorporation and the drawing up of a contract to use a painting of Bakewell Show by Sheffield artist Joe Scarborough loaned to the society, cut deeper into funds.

The 1994 show was another washout – not quite as bad as the previous year, but again it affected gate receipts and necessitated the buying of extra straw and stone and the hire of tractors. There was a valiant effort to raise extra funds by staging a barbershop concert at Lady Manners School in Bakewell in September, which raised £3,000, but support from members generally was disappointing.

Secretary Ted Brownhill retired after the show and there was a shake-up in the show office with joint directors Brian Bakel and Richard Morten playing a greater part in running the administration. Incorporation brought rationalisation and some savings, most of them one-offs, and after the 1995 show treasurer Geoff Crawford reported a profit for the first time in three years – a modest £10,419. It could have been better, but the 90-degree heat had kept people away and gate receipts were down by £19,000. However, efforts to bring the show back to its agricultural roots by creating a new agricultural quarter proved a great success with visitors who did attend.

But other issues were occupying the society; detailed consultation with Derbyshire Dales District Council over the proposed move of the livestock market onto the showground. As director Brian Bakel told the annual meeting:

The new agricultural centre... is planned to be situated on the right of our access road to the show office. It takes in the whole of that area and further across to include what is now the patrons' car park – this would necessitate the complete re-plan of the whole showground. We are working in conjunction with our landlord and our valuer to obtain the best agreement for the benefit of the society.

The following year the detailed discussions were still going on and now included the Peak Park Planning Board. Plans to bring a new road out onto the A6 before the 1997 show were still on the drawing-board and no agreements had been signed.

But all the procrastination in the world could not take away the runaway success of the show that year

The Agricultural Business Centre takes shape on the showground in 1998. (CU)

Above: *The Royal Artillery Motor Cycle Display Team.* (SN)

Right: *Shoppers find a handicraft bargain at the 1987 show.* (SN)

which saw a massive £36,500 profit. This was achieved partly thanks to extremely good attendance, but more positively from some very judicious house-keeping which had kept a tight control of the purse strings. It was also the centenary of the horticulture section, celebrated by the launch of a new competition for a scented carnation, a demonstration theatre for gardening tips and a Gardeners' Question Time.

As soon as the 1997 show closed plans were put into operation for reorganising the showground in preparation for a milestone year – probably the most significant since the show had been extended to two days 18 years previously. The development of the new Bakewell Agricultural Business Centre on the show site would launch it into a new era and give organisers the opportunity to plan for the twenty-first century.

A special committee of joint show director Richard Morten, the then-showground committee chairman Colin Underwood and showground co-ordinator Mike Patterson was set up to oversee the changes. Over the next few months the three spent many hours walking the site and measuring up, as well as talking to the different committee members to make sure everyone was happy with the new arrangements.

Main contractors Henry Boot moved onto the site at the end of September and over the next eight months worked to transform 12 acres at the top end of the showground into the new Bakewell Agricultural Business Centre. It was not easy, particularly as the end of the year brought two months of very heavy rain culminating in a very high water-table over the Christmas period. Joint Director Brian Bakel told the media at the annual press conference:

It has been hard work and we have burned a lot of midnight oil, but we believe we are now geared up to give our visitors a much bigger, better Bakewell Show. This year we are very new neighbours and have yet to explore fully the opportunities offered by the business centre; we don't expect everything to be perfect, but we are happy and confident that the future of Bakewell Show in the Millennium is very bright.

We are looking forward with great enthusiasm to this year's show and in the future to working with Derbyshire Dales District Council and the Peak District National Park Planning Authority to make better use of the showground in the rest of the year. This is the start of a new relationship between us all – it certainly gives us the opportunity to plan for the next 160 years.

In practical terms the showground had been turned around. The cattle, sheep and goats which were under canvas at the far end of the site were brought into purpose-built pens in the new centre. The dogs, pigeons and poultry which had been displaced were given a much bigger and more easily accessible area at the Haddon Road end. There was now a much bigger agricultural area with 20 per cent more trade stands. The British food and farming marquee was much bigger and had been repositioned not far from the Coombs Road entrance.

That year Bakewell Show also went on the internet. It was a curiously forward-thinking move for such a traditional organisation, which only a few years earlier had battled with fax technology, but it was seen as vital if Bakewell was to compete with the rest of the shows in Britain for visitors and attractions. The event went online in the spring, its multi-page website covering every aspect of the show from vintage vehicles to the Village Green.

❧ Six ❧

The New Millennium

When Lord Lieutenant of Derbyshire John Bather agreed to be the show's millennium president he cannot have known what a busy week it would turn out to be. For after two hectic show days performing his presidential duties he was then plunged into the county's celebrations for the Queen Mother's 100th birthday, the highlight of which was a special service at Derby Cathedral. The new president was no stranger to the show, having first attended as a young man in the 1950s when, he recalled, 'it rained a lot':

It was a very different event then with very little in the way of machinery – farmers relied on horses to do the work – and different breeds of cattle, Friesians, Shorthorns, Ayrshires, Jerseys and Guernseys, in contrast to many of the breeds shown today.

Never in my wildest dreams did I ever think I would be asked to be president of Bakewell Show, but I am absolutely delighted because it gives me the opportunity to meet a circle of people I would probably otherwise never have met.

With the Government's controversial Countryside Bill on its way through Parliament, rural issues were very high on the political agenda. The opposition Tory party saw local agricultural shows as a very good way of meeting ordinary farming folk and finding out their opinions and Bakewell was targeted for a visit by the opposition spokesman for Agricultural and Rural Affairs, Lady Byford, who had led Tory opposition to the Bill in the Commons.

The millennium brought a team of familiar voices to the showground, some of the cast of Britain's longest running radio soap for farmers, 'The Archers'. In a special 'The Archers – Roots to Radio' evening in the British food and farming marquee, avid fans of the show gathered to hear Ruth (actress Felicity Finch) and David (Timothy Bentinck), sound-effects technicians and producers uncover some of the secrets of the programme – and they even produced a cameo edition from Bakewell Show.

Meanwhile, in the horticulture marquee the show had its own version of Gardeners' Question Time with a panel of experts headed by Radio Derby's resident horticulturalist Anne Liverman.

But the 2000 show's upbeat programme hid the seriousness of the state of British farming. And the society – true to its original remit all those years ago – decided to do something to help beleaguered farmers who were finding it increasingly difficult to afford to bring their animals to the show. A decision was taken to waive the entrance fees to cattle, sheep and goat classes. As joint show director Brian Bakel commented:

We know it is only a splash in the ocean, but one we hope will make a small contribution to help ease the plight of the farmers and make them realise how much we value their attendance at the show and that we share their present problems in farming.

The society also decided to throw its weight behind the farmers' markets initiative, 'another indication of our commitment to seeing agriculture prosper in this area.' As well as being a time to look forward the millennium was a time to reflect:

We are very conscious that we are now in a new millennium and while we want to preserve the traditional aspects of Bakewell Show, which have made it such a success in the past, we know we must look to the future and the generations to come. We work hard to keep the balance between old and new and we look to improve year upon year.

When those words were spoken Brian Bakel had no idea of the impending disaster that was to hit not only the show – and almost cause only the second cancellation in its history – but the whole rural economy.

As 2001 unfolded and the first cases of foot and mouth were reported in Northumberland, there was no hint of the seriousness of what would happen. But by March show organisers were forced to hold a crisis meeting. Although no cases had been reported in Derbyshire the countryside had been effectively closed by the Government's draconian handling of the situation and the wholesale and very public burning of animal carcasses had painted a very gloomy rural picture.

Organisers had four choices. They could do what many other shows, including the Great Yorkshire and Lincolnshire had done, and cancel the 2001 event and risk losing up to £90,000 and the support of regular show-goers, or they could go ahead without livestock, which would automatically cut the number of visitors.

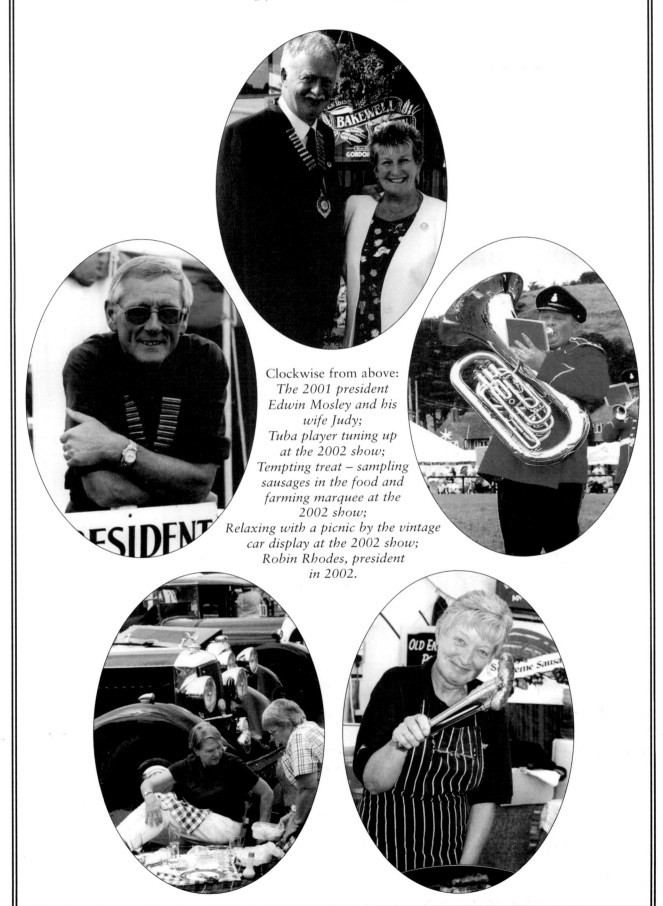

Clockwise from above:
*The 2001 president
Edwin Mosley and his
wife Judy;
Tuba player tuning up
at the 2002 show;
Tempting treat – sampling
sausages in the food and
farming marquee at the
2002 show;
Relaxing with a picnic by the vintage
car display at the 2002 show;
Robin Rhodes, president
in 2002.*

Alternatively, they could postpone the show until the situation improved, but that was an unknown factor, or they could plough ahead as usual and risk a last-minute cancellation if any cases of the disease were confirmed in the county.

It was a brave decision to go without livestock, but one which was applauded both by visitors who had been starved of country events and by trade-stand holders who were facing financial ruin having ordered all their stock before show cancellations began. Two other decisions were made: all the farmers who would, under normal circumstances, have attended the show, were sent free family tickets in the hope that they would take time off from their problems and come and have a well-deserved day out at the show, and a special 'Open for Business' marquee was erected to allow local businesses which had suffered the knock-on effects of foot and mouth to promote themselves free to the show's visitors.

The East Midlands Development Agency and the Royal Bank of Scotland came up with funding for the initiative, which proved so popular that it has continued in subsequent years. Bakewell Show 2001 was not a set-up organisers would have chosen; it was forced upon them by circumstance. But while they respected the decision of other shows to cancel, they felt that at a time when rural life was in crisis they wanted to be seen to be 'Backing the British Countryside' (which was the show's slogan that year). One final irony lay in the fact that the year when the show went ahead without livestock was the year when a working farmer was president. Edwin Mosley, who farms at Darley Dale and Snitterton, has been associated with the show since he was a boy and had stewarded in the cattle section since the early 1960s, latterly as chief cattle steward.

Hopes that the 'no livestock' show would be balanced out by a really good show in 2002 were dashed by disastrous flooding in the weeks before, sparking rumours that the weather would succeed where foot and mouth had failed in causing the cancellation of the event. Brian Bakel declared that he had never seen the showground as wet since he joined the show in 1963. Tons of woodchip, stone and gravel were tipped onto the walkways, water pumps were brought in to take away the excess water and tracking was laid in a bid to keep the car parks open. Fortunately both show days were dry and a record crowd poured through the gates, but the £25,000 bill for getting the showground ready meant that the show was a financial flop.

Much to the delight of visitors the animals were back – sadly confined to their own restricted area, which meant that the traditional Grand Parade could not take place. But the stockmen organised their own parade so the public was not disappointed. Entry numbers were good despite the problems and there is hope that they will build up again for the coming shows. Despite what fate throws at Bakewell Show, heavy rain or heatwave, disease or disaster, there is a unique spirit which always shines through. It is known as 'the friendly show', not just by visitors but also by the media, the judges and the competitors too, and it is this atmosphere which has kept the show going since it started in 1819 and will keep it going in the years to come.

Joint show director Brian Bakel being interviewed by Yorkshire Television at the 2002 show.

Millennium president John Bather presenting a trophy in the pony classes.

Promotion girls at the 2002 show.

Inspecting the steam engines at the 2002 show.

Lord Hartington accompanied by Lady Hartington presenting George Finney of Wingerworth with the Championship Shire Foal Cup, won by Wingerworth Melody, at the 1978 show. (DT)

The Duchess of Rutland admiring a display of roses in the floral-art section when her husband was president in 1960. (SN)

🍂 Seven 🍂

The Noble Connection

Bakewell Show has always enjoyed noble connections, since its very first patron, the Sixth Duke of Devonshire in 1819, to its president at the time of writing, Lord Edward Manners, brother to the Duke of Rutland. To say that the Devonshires and the Rutlands have embraced the interests of the show would be something of an understatement; over the years both families have helped keep it afloat – in the case of 1904, almost literally. Continuous rain had ruined the show, losses ran at £300 and the society had no sinking fund. The Eighth Duke of Devonshire started a relief fund, raising a useful £180 which helped stave off disaster, and this was later supplemented by a bank overdraft of £100 for which the committee stood guarantor.

Five years later cash balances were once again down to below £50 and the society was in serious danger of being wound up. Many of the farmer exhibitors rallied round and returned their prize money and the Ninth Duke of Devonshire and the Eighth Duke of Rutland generously promised to make good any deficits on the annual show for the foreseeable future.

The relationship between the society and the nobility has always been good. As early as the second show in 1820 there was concern that the local tenant farmers, unable to afford higher-quality breeding stock, might be put off entering the same classes as the Duke of Devonshire and other wealthy landowners. So they magnanimously agreed to enter their animals as 'extra stock' which meant that although they were placed by the judge they did not qualify for prize money.

There were other benefits to this mutual understanding. In 1826 the president was Sir George Crewe of Calke Abbey in the south of the county. At the annual dinner that year guests dined on what the *Derby Mercury* described as 'uncommonly fine buck provided by the president from his herd at Calke, along with a splendid basket of fresh caught trout

The Duchess of Rutland presenting a prize to a winner in the horse class in 1960.

given by the Duke of Rutland.' Indeed, the Dukes of Rutland and Devonshire both generously provided venison, game and fish for the annual dinners throughout the nineteenth century.

The Duke of Rutland was indirectly involved in the show's next milestone. By 1827 the society had grown to such an extent, attracting members from all over the country, that it was decided to change its name to Derbyshire Agricultural Society. It was soon after this that the Duke built a new Cattle Market in Bakewell which proved a much larger and more appropriate venue for alternate show years than the grounds around the Rutland Arms.

Fourteen years later, when the presidency of railway pioneer George Stephenson saw a shift of emphasis towards new implements and new farm machinery, the show moved temporarily to Chatsworth Park. There, at the Edensor end of the park, all sorts of farming machinery, from a paring plough and clod breaker to turnip and chaff cutters and a new kind of cheese press, was put on display. The Duke of Devonshire had his new threshing-machine by Garratt of Leiston, Suffolk, on view and working, which according to a local press report 'heralded the end of winnowing corn with flails on the barn floor.'

The society often went back to Chatsworth Park after that, particularly when there were large exhibitions of machinery which needed more space.

The 1840s – one of the most progressive periods in Britain's agricultural history – saw the Dukes and the wealthy landowners unwittingly embroiled in a split which was to end with the original society being swallowed up by the new tenant-farmer-led Bakewell Farmers' Club formed by brothers Peter and Lawrence Furniss in 1843. The club was established because Lawrence Furniss thought the aristocracy had too much power and wanted the farmers to be more in control and in touch with the revolution taking place in agriculture at the time.

37

Above: *Prime Minister Harold MacMillan and visitors at the 1960 show.*

Above inset: *Lady Hilton* (centre) *during her presidential year with Lord Granby, later Duke of Rutland* (left) *and joint show director Brian Bakel* (right).

Right: *The 2003 president Lord Edward Manners.* (CU)

The Duchess of Rutland presenting the trophy to the champion bull at the 1991 show. (CU)

The Duchess of Rutland accepts a special rod given to her by Fisherman's Walk chairman Graham Walmsley, watched by Brian Bakel. (CU)

Far right: *The Duchess of Rutland with show secretary Bill Conway in 1960.*

Right: *The Duke of Rutland presenting a cup to a prizewinning sheep from the Loynton flock in 1999.* (CU)

Below: *The Marquis and Marchioness of Hartington watching centre-ring attractions with director John Smallman* (left), *Sally Smallman* (right) *and show historian Lance Waud* (slightly obscured) *at the 1985 show.* (CU)

Below: *Prime Minister Harold MacMillan with the Duchess of Devonshire at the 1960 show.*

(McC)

Below: *The Duchess of Rutland during her presidency in 1991 with the Duke* (right), *Brian Bakel* (left) *and Brian Monaghan, chairman of the horticulture committee.* (CU)

Right: *President the Earl of Burlington strokes a prize bull at the 1996 show; his sister Lady Jasmine is pictured* (right) *with the trophy.* (CU)

From small beginnings the club began to develop initially as a discussion society. Meanwhile the North Derbyshire Society still held its shows, enthusiastically supported by the Duke of Devonshire who at one show brought along an extra 67 of his finest animals for visitors to see. Then the club stopped merely talking and decided to stage a modest event, much to the disapproval of the society. Initially the majority of society members did not support it, but by the fourth show in 1852 records show that the Duke of Devonshire and other landowners were showing their stock. An attempt by the society to get Bakewell Farmers' Club and other smaller clubs which had sprung up to affiliate with what they saw as the parent body was met with a blank wall and the society reacted by changing its name again to Chesterfield and North East Derbyshire Agricultural Society and holding its own show in Chesterfield.

Meanwhile Bakewell Farmers' Club was flourishing and by 1861, following its 13th show, the rift with the society appeared to have healed. Many of the landowners who had originally spurned the new club had now become part of it. Records do not show an actual break in terms of staging the annual show, but more the overtaking of one organisation by another. But in the latter part of the nineteenth century the driving force behind Bakewell Show was unquestionably the Farmers' Club.

No matter who was running the show, the Dukes continued to support it with enthusiasm. When in 1878 a dog section was introduced Lord George Cavendish MP (president in 1835 and again in 1852) brought along five gun dogs, two retrievers and three setters, not for competition, but to show visitors.

Lord George proved a worthy champion for farmers in Parliament. Both he and the Duke of Rutland had made strong pleas for more positive protection for agriculture. On one of his rare visits to the annual show dinner in 1879, held in a marquee on the showground with catering by Thomas Higgott of the Red Lion Hotel, the Duke gave a wide-ranging speech on the problems, both national and international, which were threatening to lead farming into yet another serious depression. He was particularly concerned about competition from abroad. Several fledgling Derbyshire cheese factories had closed as a result of importing cheese from America, and the repeal of the Corn Laws had pushed the decline of farming even further.

The 1879 show was another landmark in the show's history because it was staged on a spacious piece of ground called Twenty Acres on Belper Road – this is thought by Lance Waud to be the present Recreation Ground, given to the town by the Duke of Rutland in 1885 together with a large field to the south, which has since been developed for housing.

Eleven years later in 1890 the show welcomed the new Duke of Rutland as a visitor. He had just succeeded to the title and the lands and as a previous

President the Earl of Burlington meets rabbit committee chairman Ken Watts at the 1996 show. (CU)

show president, when he was the Marquis of Granby, he was keen to continue the patronage.

Records show that he was greeted enthusiastically by the large crowd, listened to selections from Birchover Brass Band and tucked into the show dinner of salmon, roast chicken and duck, cold rib of beef and leg of lamb, york ham and ox tongue, sweets and the first-prize Derby cheese from that day's show.

As the new century dawned the Devonshires and the Rutlands maintained their involvement, backing the society with financial guarantees and making up shortfalls to help keep it going. It is not documented to what extent they subsidised the show, but between 1910 and 1914, with the exception of 1913, gate receipts together with the sale of catalogues and the parking of carriages did not cover the prize money.

One condition of their support was that they should be represented on the show's committee – and this led to the active involvement of key people from both estates, usually the agents. Certainly in the case of Chatsworth this was to have a practical benefit, for after the war much of the administration for the show was carried out in the estate offices. The Duke of Devonshire's agent Roland Burke, later to become Sir Roland Burke, was a particular stalwart of the show. He worked hard on its behalf and in 1920 became director, a post he held for ten years, relinquishing it only because of his appointment as Director of the Royal Show.

Both Dukes are still represented on the show council today, although it is not necessarily any longer the role of the agent. The Dukes of Devonshire and Rutland jointly held the presidency during the war years, 1914–18, when the society continued to meet spasmodically (although there were no shows until 1920). The following year the Marquis of Hartington was president. The 1933 show was distinctive for a particularly 'blue-blooded' reason. The previous year King George V won the Bakewell Challenge Cup outright for his colt foal out of a six-year-old mare called Pendley Choice. He was delighted and his private secretary wrote to the committee saying the King wanted to re-present the cup freshly inscribed 'HM the King's Champion Challenge Cup' for the best colt or filly foal in the show. Naturally they accepted his offer and the cup in its new form was presented for the first time at the 1933 show. Seventy years later the cup remains one of the society's most precious trophies. In the last few years honours have been shared evenly between the Yateses of Farnah House Farm, Duffield, and the Mosses of Hillmoor Farm, Eaton, near Congleton in Cheshire.

In 1936, by which time the show was being run by the renamed Bakewell Agricultural and Horticultural Society, the Marchioness of Hartington was president. The following year the Ninth Duke of Devonshire took the reins again for the fifth time and in 1938 it was the turn of the Ninth Duke of Rutland.

It was when the show resumed in 1946, with the Marquis of Hartington as president, that the current Duchess of Devonshire, formerly Lady Andrew following her marriage to Andrew Cavendish (and then Marchioness of Huntington following her brother-in-law's death in 1944), remembers her first visit:

We were living at The Rookery at Ashford in the Water at the time. There was a great family tradition of attending Bakewell Show. It was very highly thought of both by my father-in-law the Duke and by his agent.

But she probably remembers her second visit better, recalled by many as 'Lady Andrew's year' in deference to a beautiful light-bay Hackney mare standing at 15.1 hands, who made her debut. Bred at Mrs Edgar Henrique's stud at Southport and originally named Violetta by previous owners, she was bought by the current Duchess of Devonshire, who later sold her to keen Hackney enthusiast and long-time show supporter George Daybell. It was he who, in tribute to Lady Andrew), re-registered the horse with its new name. Between 1947 and 1951 won 21 championships at all the major shows and was champion for five years at Bakewell – her home show.

The Duchess believes that over the years the Chatsworth estate would have entered Jerseys and Simmenthals and probably some Jacob sheep under the watchful eye of farm manager John McLaughlin who she describes as 'a very powerful and authoritative figure'. It was not unusual for the animals to be walked to the show – unlike today, there weren't many cattle trucks around.

The Duchess' husband's aunt, Lady Maud Baillie of Ashford Hall (president in 1930, three years after her husband Captain, the Hon. Evan Baillie), a stalwart of the High Peak Harriers, would parade her hounds, and she recalls that her sisters-in-law Lady Elizabeth and Lady Anne Cavendish would enter the pony classes and often win cups 'which they probably still have'.

The Shire horses were a particularly spectacular sight at the show. The powerhouse of the farm, she says, they were looked after by Tommy Jones. Out of show time Tommy Jones would walk the Shires to neighbouring farms for stud duty. The Dukes considered it their responsibility to keep a good strong line going. The Duchess continues:

Bakewell Show was something we looked forward to very much. Judges and other people who came to the show would come and stay with us – we were very proud that we had one of the finest one-day shows in England. We used to spend the whole day there and as soon as we arrived we'd go to the stands. I shall always remember the tables in the centre ring laden with trophies and the wonderful highlight of the Grand Parade.

The Tenth Duke of Devonshire was president in 1949 and sadly a year later he died. As a mark of respect the society cancelled its annual dinner and donated £5 to the Royal Masonic Hospital in lieu of a wreath. The new Duke and Duchess continued to carry the family baton.

The 1955 show proved a right royal year. Britain's new young Queen entered Red Poll cattle from her Sandringham estate in the livestock classes – the first time that a reigning monarch had exhibited in cattle classes at the show. And they proved a winner. Royal Gloxina took first prize in her class and Royal Gypsy came away with a third-place rosette. The following year Her Majesty was even more successful, carrying off three firsts, again with her Red Polls.

In 1961 the Queen's horse Imperial was among metropolitan horses at the show, the same year that Government business kept the president from attending. The Duke of Devonshire had an unexpected political engagement connected with his office of Under Secretary for Commonwealth Relations and he expressed bitter disappointment and sent profound apologies... and the Duchess to preside over the official show lunch.

The previous year the Prime Minister Harold MacMillan had been a guest at the show causing the *Derbyshire Times* to remark: 'It is an odd twist that state affairs should have detained the Duke – for at last year's show the Prime Minister managed to relax from Government affairs.'

The Devonshires' young family were keen supporters of the show; in 1952 their son, the Marquis of Hartington, came third in the hunter classes, and in 1965 their daughter, Lady Sophie Cavendish, made her debut with a Shetland pony. She was one of the youngest exhibitors and carried off first prize in the Mountain and Moorland section with Chatsworth Easter Bonnet. Lady Sophie was clearly following a family trend – at the 1981 show the *Sheffield Star* reported:

Appropriately dressed in yachting cap, triple strand of pearls and wellington boots, the Duchess won every Shetland class except the yearling colts and fillies, the one for which she had donated the prize money.

One of the highlights of the late 1960s was the appearance of the Duke of Devonshire's great racing mare Park Top at the 1969 show. Fresh from her triumph in the King George VI and Queen Elizabeth Diamond Stakes at Ascot, Park Top was paraded around the centre ring by an apprentice jockey in the Duke's racing silks while he gave a commentary on her remarkable achievements on the race track. Mary Daybell, president in 1981, remembers it well: 'It was such a thrill. Park Top was a real personality, and we were delighted to see her.'

Both the Rutlands and the Devonshires continued their support for the show, but it is the Duchess of Devonshire, a regular visitor and exhibitor at the show, as well as president in 1954 and 1969, who has made her affection for the show, and the farming community it represents, particularly clear. In 1978 when her son the Marquis of Hartington was president she told the *Sheffield Star*:

It's a great day at Bakewell, the showground is delightful and there is such a varied programme. As it is so close to Chatsworth I feel wonderfully at home. I would rather be with farmers than any other breed of human. I feel completely at home with them. I like their attitude to life and admire their constant battle with nature.

The Duke of Devonshire had cause to remember that year with slightly less affection. According to the report in the *Derbyshire Times* he had to abandon his chauffeur-driven car in the traffic jam and take a brisk walk to the showground. He was late arriving for a radio show and later took a mud bath after falling off a chair! Over the years the Duchess has seen many changes, some of which her forefathers would have approved and others which they would have been less enthusiastic about:

Several things have come to the fore in recent years – the cheese tent, poultry and eggs and food and farming – all of which I think are vital. We need to show young people where things come from and how important British farming is today.

Regarding the thrusting new commercial emphasis she is quite philosophical: 'I think my grandfather-in-law would have been saddened to see it, but I think my father-in-law would just have accepted it was part of the changing world.'

One thing which makes the Duchess such a popular figure is her willingness to embrace the show 'on the ground', as it were. It is not unusual to see her plodding around the showground in her wellies as the final preparations are taking place, and one year when she had forgotten her official passes – she's an honorary life patron – she willingly paid to come in when an over-zealous gateman, who didn't realise who she was, refused her entrance.

The latter part of the century saw a European royal take part in the show. King Olaf of Norway's daughter, Princess Martha Louise (who was studying in Britain), twice competed against 35 of the top 100 showjumpers in the country on her horses Persimmon and Caybareen. Unfortunately she failed to qualify for the Horse of the Year Show at Wembley: 'I'm disappointed,' she told the *Sheffield Star* at the time, 'but I'm going to cheer myself up with some Bakewell pudding later.'

The Devonshires and Rutlands have continued to play a part in the show, even to the point of persuading the newer and less familiar members of their families to be president. The Dowager Duchess of Rutland was a self-confessed city girl before she met the Duke and admits that when they married she had no idea about country life. So when she was first approached to follow in her husband's presidential footsteps she declined the offer. But when they asked a second time in 1991 she thought 'why not?' and accepted, delighted to follow in a proud family tradition, which had seen her husband the Tenth Duke acting as president three times, in 1947, 1960 and 1972.

She said she was pleased to see the way in which the show was building on the good things of the past and introducing new ideas to ensure the event's survival in the future, adding: 'Bakewell Show has a unique atmosphere which fosters friendships old and new.' When her son became the Eleventh Duke on the death of his father he too became president, telling visitors at the time:

My family at Haddon Hall has had a long and happy association with the county. We always spend our August holiday at Haddon fishing and taking an interest in the estate and local activities. I spent many happy August days attending the show as a child with my brothers and sisters.

At the tender age of 27, William, Earl of Burlington, was the youngest ever president, but he said he felt a great pride at being associated with what he considered to be 'a rural masterpiece'. He was also proud to be carrying on an old family tradition – both his grandparents, the Duke and Duchess of Devonshire, and his parents, the Marquis and Marchioness of Hartington, had held the position before him. William was one of the new breed of nobility – described at the time as 'a normal fun-loving young man who cooks curry, holds a season ticket for Arsenal and who loves to travel.' But despite the fact that he chose to be a working photographer rather than an archetypal aristocrat, it was an inspired choice by the society. William's obvious respect for the show was a good sign that the younger generation was ready to stake their claim and accept that the continuation of the event rested on their shoulders.

✿ Eight ✿

Show People and Their Memories

Even from its earliest beginnings Bakewell Show has relied heavily on an army of willing volunteers – people without whom the show could not go on. And records show that for many people, particularly the farmers, it was a family affair handed down from generation to generation. In this chapter we look at some of the characters who have helped shape the show and examine the lasting legacy they have left behind.

Wootten Thomas will go down in history as the founding father of Bakewell Show. It was he who, concerned at the state of British farming, called the inaugural meeting and became the first president. A well-known Chesterfield lawyer, Wootten Thomas was involved in a number of local projects. He was secretary to the Turnpike Trust which was building roads in the county, and was also a leading light in the building of St Thomas' Church on Chatsworth Road in Chesterfield. But it was his farming interests which drove him to try to help the poor, beleaguered farmers back in 1819.

He was a progressive farmer with 800 acres of land in Boythorpe, Brampton and Walton. He specialised in Merino sheep and regularly attended shearings at Holkham and Woburn – indeed his reputation was such that he exchanged breeding sheep with King George III. One of the first farmers in Derbyshire to hold demonstrations on his own farm, it is reported that he, his family and all his farm workers wore clothes made from cloth spun from the backs of his own sheep. But it was not only his sheep for which he was renowned; he took the prize for the best bull in the United Kingdom at Aldridge's Repository in London in 1821 when he was awarded the Board of Agriculture's silver cup worth 30 guineas.

His bull, King Charles II, was named champion at the first Bakewell Show. Two years later, when it weighed a massive 1 ton 2³/₄ cwts (1,548 lbs), it again won him the silver cup at Islington for the best bull in the United Kingdom. The beast, which stood 5ft 3ins tall, was a cross between a Shorthorn and an ancestral Longhorn. It was finally slaughtered in Chesterfield on 19 December 1821 when it was five years old.

It was not only his livestock that was valued – Wootten Thomas' farm won the Board of Agriculture's special award of a silver vase worth 30 guineas for the best cultivated farm in the society's district at the 1821 show.

The last mention made of him in Lance Waud's book is in reference to the 1834 society dinner. By now in failing health, he replied to a toast to 'the father of the society' by rejoicing to see the society rich in assets, but regretting that so many members were behind in their subscriptions.

Lawrence Furniss was the next figurehead to dominate the society, but for a quite different reason. A working farmer (with his brother Peter he farmed Birchill's Farm near Bakewell and in the village of Pilsley), Lawrence Furniss believed that North Derbyshire Agricultural Society, of which he was a member, had become too far removed from the ordinary man and that the gentry had too much control. He was also a member of the Royal Agricultural Society of England and helped organise the Royal Shows when they were staged in Derby. That role brought him into contact with other forward-thinking farmers and scientists who were not only doing some wonderful work, but showed him that an agricultural revolution was taking place, and he did not want to be left behind.

Lawrence Furniss' dream was to set up an organisation which more clearly met his needs – a forum where farmers could meet together and learn about technical progress from scientists and leading farmers. He also wanted to set up a library containing all the latest information. The brothers called a meeting, the result of which was the setting up of Bakewell Farmers' Club, which ran in tandem with North Derbyshire Society for a good number of years. It was only when the club stopped being a debating society and decided to stage an annual show that the cracks in the relationship between the two organisations began to appear. Some five years later the two organisations merged and formed the foundation of the society as it is today.

The involvement in a traditional agricultural show of railway pioneer, **George Stephenson**, would seem to be curious, until one considers the revolution which was taking place in the world of farm machinery at the time. In 1838 George Stephenson, who lived at Tapton House in Chesterfield, was the chief guest at the show and the dinner. He made a lengthy speech, wherein, having disclaimed all knowledge of agriculture, he went on to talk powerfully about the benefits of land drainage based on observations he had made

Clockwise
from above:
*Former president and lifelong
supporter Sandy Caudwell* (CU);
Wendy Rhodes (CU);
*Dorrie Patterson – to be
president in 2004* (CU);
*Ted Brownhill, secretary from
1976 to 1994;
Charles Mycock, chief livestock steward* (CU);
*Joint show director Richard
Morten* (CU);
Mary Morten (CU).

in East Lothian and in Belgium while pioneering his railway systems. He told the assembled company how water moved in the soil and described the effect of water-logging on the plant's root system. He went on to outline the kind of drain tiles which should be used, their layout, depth, spacing and so on.

The speech received a standing ovation and prompted the society to give a prize for the most successful example of field drainage on farms of varying sizes in the area, the following year. This competition continued until the county was largely drained. So impressed was the society with George Stephenson that they asked him to be president in 1841 – appropriately the year when the venue changed to Chatsworth Park to accommodate the different kinds of pioneering agricultural machinery which went on show. He made another long speech at the dinner – this time concerning the application of science and agriculture, in particular how he thought Derbyshire farmers might improve their growth of potatoes and fodder root crops.

Seven years later, just days after the show, George Stephenson, arguably the most internationally renowned of all the event's presidents, died.

Only one person has enjoyed the distinction of being president of Bakewell Show four times, a Mr **R.W.M. Nesfield**, who held office in 1853, 1865, 1869 and 1901, when he completed 50 years' membership of the society. One of the best known and highly respected men in Bakewell, Mr Nesfield was land agent to the Duke of Rutland for more than half a century. He was master of the High Peak Hunt for 35 years, during which he had ridden all the land for miles around Bakewell. He was chairman of the bench for a similar period and president of many other bodies. According to Lance Waud, the 1905 president, the Duke of Rutland, travelling to the show from Longshaw Lodge, called to see his old friend at Castle Hill on the way there and again on his way back, but arrived too late. Curiously Mr Nesfield, aged 90, had died on show day.

Roland Burke was the Duke of Devonshire's land agent who became involved with the show when the Duke and the Duke of Rutland offered to underwrite the show's losses in return for playing a more active role in running the event. Much of the administration was carried out from the estate offices and Roland Burke was very much involved, taking over as director in 1920. He was instrumental in acquiring the Twenty Acres adjacent to Coombs Road, which gave the show a great deal more space, and is credited with organising a brilliant event in 1926, despite the gloom of the General Strike that year. But Roland Burke was destined for greater things. After ten years as director of Bakewell Show he was offered the prestigious job of director to the Royal Show. It was a blow to Bakewell but led to Sir Roland – as he was later to become – making a lasting mark on agriculture in this country. Despite moving to Woodbridge in Suffolk, Sir Roland

kept his interest in Bakewell alive; he was show president three times, in 1925, 1939 and again in 1955. And when he and Lady Burke celebrated their golden wedding anniversary in 1955 the society presented them with an inscribed album and a weather vane for the roof of their home to remind them of his association with Bakewell Show.

Sir Roland stepped down from the Royal Show in 1950, when artist Oswald Birley was commissioned to paint a full-length portrait of him, which still has pride of place at the Royal Agricultural Society for England headquarters at Stoneleigh in Warwickshire. Indeed, such was Sir Roland's impact on agricultural shows nationally that the RASE still presents three trophies in his name – for the best pair of beef animals (same breed), the best pair of dairy animals (same breed) and the Perpetual Challenge Machinery Trophy, much coveted by Britain's farm-machinery manufacturers.

Fourteen years after his father had the honour, **Capt. the Rt Hon. Charles Waterhouse** of Middleton Hall became president when the society resumed activities after the First World War. He was to go on and be president twice more – in 1948 and in 1966. An indefatigable worker, he was a member of the show committee for a number of years and in recognition of his work was only the second person to be made an Honorary Life Member. He became a Tory MP in 1924 and served firstly for South Leicester and later, after boundaries were changed, for Leicester South East, retiring in 1957 to pursue his business interests in Africa (where he was chairman of Tanganyika Concessions). During his career he held a number of Government posts including Assistant Postmaster General and Parliamentary Secretary to the Board of Trade. He was also Magistrate and Deputy Lieutenant for the county. The committee stood as a mark of respect when he died in 1975. Fourteen years later his son Major Hugo Waterhouse was to follow in the footsteps of his father and grandfather and become president of the show too.

Matthew Longson has his own personal chapter in Bakewell Show history, having been honorary show director for 17 years from 1958 to 1975, the longest period so far held by any show director. Before that he was honorary treasurer for eight years and his quarter of a century's active involvement was rewarded with Life Membership of the society. Matthew Longson became closely associated with the show after being appointed manager of the local branch of Williams Deacons Ltd (Williams and Glyns Bank) in 1949. But his memories of the Little Royal go back much further. He remembered travelling by train from his home at Chapel-en-le-Frith with his father to visit Bakewell Show as a schoolboy in the early part of the century:

My father was a poultry man and a keen exhibitor in a number of shows. One way and another I seem to have been mixed up with agricultural shows for most of my life.

That includes Staffordshire County Show with which he was involved during 21 years as a bank manager in Uttoxeter before moving to Bakewell.

His term of office as show director coincided with an era of ambitious and buoyant expansion after a decade of successful consolidation in the postwar years. Metal roads were laid on the showground, a drainage system was installed and the secretary's office transferred from the market-place to a new permanent building on the showground and many other improvements carried out. One of his particular interests was the horticultural trade section and he played a major part in attracting the interest of the country's leading firms. And Matthew Longson had the distinction of welcoming Prime Minister Harold MacMillan to the show in 1960 and accompanying the premier on a tour of the ground:

It was a proud and happy day for Bakewell Show and Mr MacMillan later wrote to me thanking the society for their hospitality and saying how much he'd enjoyed the visit.

Lance Waud, for many years the Ministry of Agriculture Advisory Officer for North Derbyshire, was also an enthusiastic local historian, who produced histories of Derbyshire Agricultural and Horticultural Society, Ashover Show and Brailsford Ploughing and Hedge-Cutting Association before tackling one of Bakewell Show in 1989.

It was he who would uncover the discrepancies in Bakewell Show dates – accounting for the sudden leap from the 137th to the 159th show – and challenged the 'mistake' theory on the creation of Bakewell pudding. He found evidence that it was on the menu for a show dinner a good 20 years before it was deemed to have been 'invented'.

Lance Waud was a farmer's man, friendly and knowledgeable, and during his time with the ministry he persuaded and encouraged farmers to change their habits and methods and improve production. As a farmer's son he could talk from personal knowledge. He had a proud boast that he had been on every farm in North Derbyshire and in most of the fields. When he wasn't writing history books Lance Waud enjoyed singing (he was a good bass singer) and was much sought after as a speaker at all sorts of occasions.

Frank Twiggs, dog-show chairman for 25 years and honorary life member from 1967, had another reason to thank Bakewell Show... he met his wife Joyce at the 1973 event. Frank first attended when he entered his cocker spaniel in 1936 and by the time of his retirement in 1992 he had successfully built up dog show numbers to more than 2,000.

Ted Brownhill was the show secretary who steered the event to two days – which seems curious since his background was anything but agricultural. But what Ted lacked in farming know-how he more than made up for in organisational skills. A would-be footballer who was on Sheffield United's books until his call-up, he became a cadet at Sandhurst where he passed as one of the top six cadets from that intake of 120. He joined the York and Lancaster Regiment and served in Egypt, North Africa, Greece and Malta. When the war was over he returned to his job in the steel industry, but with his interest in sport soon became involved in the welfare side of the company. He spent eight years in charge of Davy United's sports and social centre in Sheffield and then had a complete change when he went to serve as manager of Abbeydale Golf Club.

When the job as secretary of Bakewell Show was advertised he was ready for a change and stumbled upon the vocation he'd been searching for for 35 years. During his tenure, which ended in 1994 after 19 years, Ted oversaw heatwaves and downpours, financial triumphs and disasters, and looked after presidents from working farmers to noble Dukes and Duchesses. One of his earliest and, he said, fondest memories was attending his first general committee meeting and seeing the Duchess of Devonshire on her hands and knees poring over a map of the showground and describing how she thought the Grand Parade should take place. The decision to go to two days in 1979 was, he said, inevitable:

I rehatched a scheme that had been proposed several years before, brought it up to date and we had a two-day show. Looking back it was the only way we could save the show. It meant we could get two bites at attendance and at the weather, because more often than not we had one glorious day and one not-so-glorious.

Ted, with his trademark pipe, which he puffed through every crisis, slept in the office during the show so that he could be ready at 7a.m. when he went on the loud-speaker to welcome everyone, give a time check and a weather forecast. And when it was over he spoke for the rest of the army of volunteers: 'Probably the worst time is the morning after when, no matter how successful the show has been, you feel totally deflated and sad that it's over for another year.'

The Morten family, who farmed 220 acres at Cowdale near Buxton, have been associated with Bakewell Show for several generations and Richard Morten, the joint director in 2003, is married to the former Mary Elliott, whose family are also stalwarts of the show. Not surprisingly the couple met as Young Farmers. He was president in 1993, following in the footsteps of his father Donald who held office in 1977. Richard's great-grandfather (also Richard) and his grandfather John both used to show Shorthorn cattle at the show, although it seems it was rather more for fun than serious competition. In his memoirs Donald says he was never an exhibitor or 'showman' in that sense, but has always been a supporter of the show. He said:

The earliest memory I have was going with father and I think the show was then on the Recreation Ground.

The first time I took part was when I was connected with the Ministry of Agriculture. We put on quite a large advisory stand at the end of the war when farmers and food were badly needed. Quantity came first, quality followed later. Artificial insemination was in its infancy, tuberculin testing of cattle was being encouraged, contagious abortion elimination was only being thought about, hybrid pigs and poultry were still a dream for the future. Milk hygiene was in the front line and a large proportion of cows were still hand milked.

Not long after he became involved with the event in the early 1960s, Donald was invited to join the show committee and then to be a steward on the Dairy Shorthorn section of the cattle. When Eddie Caudwell retired as chief cattle steward in the early 1970s, Arthur Elliott (Mary's father) held the post for a brief time before he was taken ill, when Donald was asked to take over.

Donald, who was show president in 1977, retained his chief stewardship of the cattle, sheep and goats for about 15 years until he retired and handed over to Edwin Mosley. But he continued to go into the show office each Monday market day to 'offer advice to his successor'. Donald died in August 2000.

Richard Morten's earliest memories of the show date back to when he was a toddler – so eager to get into the ground that he found himself holding the hand of a complete stranger. 'I was so embarrassed,' he recalls. Every year Richard went to the show with his father and when he was old enough he would help with the cattle stewarding. He was involved in the first Young Farmers' cavalcade in 1967 and shortly afterwards was asked to be a cattle steward. He had that job for a short time then he moved on to the centre ring working with Brian Bakel, until he became deputy director – something he has continued to do since the pair were appointed joint directors following incorporation. Mary was also involved in the first YFC cavalcade, mostly making costumes with a lady called Miss Spooner from Baslow, but it is with the food and farming exhibition that she has made her mark. She became involved when it was launched in 1989, was committee chairman for a number of years and still organises the specialist cheese-making competition. And now Richard and Mary have passed on their interest to their daughter Tricia who, after working in the show office for several years, has become a trade stand steward.

The Mycock family too have staked a very firm claim in the future. They have lived at Town Head Farm in Flagg since 1903 and can trace their association with the show back to the early 1900s when Joseph Mycock served on the committee. Indeed, the

William Mycock (right) sorting out the livestock entries. (DT)

family's name is indelibly written on the show's history as the outright winner of the Thorneycroft Cup in 1927 with a Shorthorn bull. Joseph's interest was passed on to his son Thomas who used to exhibit Shorthorns and it was Thomas who took his son William to his first Bakewell Show in the early 1930s: 'I can't remember a deal about it, just that my father put me in a little mac and sou'wester and took me along. It obviously rained in those days too.' William didn't get properly involved until after the war when the Young Farmers' Club members were approached and asked to become stewards. Together with Mary Daybell and another show stalwart, Glover Broome, he volunteered and has been associated with the show ever since.

Picking up the pieces after the war wasn't easy with food and petrol rationing still in operation, but they had a few local tents, together with machinery men and animal-feed merchants. In those days the cattle were mainly Herefords and Angus with no continental breeds. Being a working farmer with his own pedigree herd – the Flagg Herd – William naturally gravitated towards the livestock section, a mantle which has since been taken over by his son Charles who, after a number of years stewarding in the cattle pens, is now chief steward, which caused a little family amusement when he found himself giving orders to his father. Charles is also on the show management committee. Brother David is involved in the cattle lines too and has served on the show's finance committee.

The Caudwell family could also be said to be classic 'show stock'. Eddie Caudwell, a working farmer who also ran Caudwell's Mill at Rowsley, was assistant show director for a number of years as well as chief cattle steward. His long service was recognised in 1972 when he was elected an honorary life member of the show. He was a competitor too and grew exquisite sweet peas which he used to show. His wife Minnie was the doyenne of the horticulture marquee, which clearly influenced her twin sons Sandy and Ian who have helped at the show from an early age. They first went in 1946 when they were just six and they have been going ever since. When they grew older they took on responsibility for setting up the horticulture tent and marking out the bays and managed to find a way of boosting their pocket money in the process. They had seen exhibits sold after the show which caused them to scour the garden for anything they could find and enter every class they could – working on the premise that the more they entered the more they could sell.

At 14 Sandy became the youngest person to be elected on to the horticulture committee and later became a member of the general committee at the start of what was to be a lifelong connection with the show. When he and Ian finished their training at Harper Adams Agricultural College, Ian worked on the family farm and Sandy went to the mill. Being a working

farmer didn't leave Ian a lot of time to help, indeed Sandy was often to be seen at Hall Farm helping with the shearing and harvesting. But Sandy's job first at the mill and later as area sales manager in a waste-compacting business was flexible enough to allow him to be involved. One of his jobs was as show commentator – following in the footsteps of professional Raymond Brooks-Ward. He might have been a hard act to follow, but Sandy handled it superbly and soon became the voice of the show. And on one occasion in the 1980s he was called upon to deal with a situation which even Raymond Brooks-Ward would have found challenging. A Limousin bull, thought to have been spooked by a dog in the crowd, escaped from the Grand Parade, and while he didn't exactly run amok, he was a hefty beast trotting in and out of the crowd. Sandy kept up his commentary, calming the crowd and reassuring them while the handlers tried to get hold of the animal. It eventually stopped right in front of the Pony Club children who were staying absolutely still – just as he'd told them to. His other job was as chief recording steward for livestock, which involved getting all of the class winners from the judges, putting them in order, sorting out the names of the cup winners and relaying all the information to the show office.

Both Sandy – president in 1995 – and Ian are still involved in the society as serving members of the council, and over the last two decades Sandy has been involved in many of the major decisions which have been taken. He is currently on the show management committee and chairman of both the finance and general committees, and has also been heavily involved in the fund-raising and events committee, helping to organise quizzes, concerts and antiques fairs to raise money for the show.

The Mosley family too have enjoyed a long association with Bakewell Show which began when Edwin Mosley, who had Highfields Farm at Ashford, first became involved before the war. He was the grandfather of the Edwin Mosley who was president in 2001 and who still plays an active part as vice-chairman of the livestock committee. Edwin senr's son Percy (Edwin junr's father) used to steward at the show and as a youngster Edwin junr would go along to help, which is where he first developed his interest in rare breeds – particularly Dexter cattle.

Percy was a contemporary of his cousin Clifford Mosley, president in 1974, during whose year a special garden party was organised at Alton Manor, home of Col Peter Hilton, which raised £275 for show funds. Clifford Mosley was an active member of the show throughout his life and was rewarded with a life membership in the mid-1970s. Clifford's widow Doris Mosley is still an active supporter of the show.

Edwin junr would probably have stayed as a cattle steward, but for the early death of his father, when it was suggested – by Donald Morten, then vice-chairman of the livestock committee – that he should

Cheers! Edwin Mosley, president in 2001 (left), with *Donald Morten, president in 1977, Brian Monaghan, chairman of the horticulture committee, and Cath Morten at the president's reception.* (CU)

carry on the family tradition and join the livestock committee. 'Those were the days when Charles Waterhouse, Col Wise and Matthew Longson were in charge and what they said went,' Edwin recalls. When Arthur Elliott retired as chairman of the livestock committee, Donald Morten took over and Edwin became vice-chairman. Then when Donald Morten retired, Edwin took over the top job, which he continued to do until he became president, when he handed over to Charles Mycock.

Charles still holds the reins and Edwin has become vice-chairman. It was a sad irony that with his long connection with livestock, Edwin should have been president in the year when foot and mouth kept all animals off the showground.

Edwin has now moved back to Snitterton, where he was born and bred. He farms there with his brothers Chris and Nick as well as at Darley Dale. They rear lambs and cattle which they sell on for someone else to fatten up. Chris does not have as high a profile role in the show as Edwin but he does do some stewarding and has been involved in sheep judging. What makes Bakewell Show special for Edwin, one of the few working farmers involved in the organisation? 'I enjoy the competition. Seeing the very best animals – that's what we all strive to achieve at home on a commercial farm.'

Mary Daybell was the first woman to be chosen from 'the ranks' to be president of the show, and more than 20 years on she is still an enthusiastic supporter, although now her contribution is limited to going into the centre ring to hand out the rosettes in the Hackney classes. She well remembers being taken to the show as a child by her father, Ashford farmer George Daybell, an active supporter who worked tirelessly for the show and was later to be made one of the society's first honorary life members:

From childhood I was indoctrinated by my father that Bakewell Show was special and not to be missed. To be allowed to help in any way was a great privilege as well as a pleasure.

I attended the 1924 show when Mr Tinsley of Ashford was president, and apart from two years when I was training in London, it is possible I have attended every show since.

When the show was revived in 1946 George Daybell asked the committee to reintroduce Hackney classes. He became chief steward and his daughter, her uncle, Ralph Warrington, and later Fred Rodgers from Clowne, became his assistants. Miss Daybell also stewarded the private driving and light trade turnout classes until the show became a two-day event. Shortage of petrol during the war years meant driving horses and ponies had become very popular. George Daybell bought and sold them and exhibited them at small shows and gymkhanas, raising money for charity. One such purchase was a beautiful bay mare which he sold to today's Duchess of Devonshire – then Lady Andrew Cavendish – who lived in the same village, Ashford in the Water. George Daybell showed the mare for her new owner at small shows and events and, on Lord William Cavendish's death in action, she became Lady Hartington and sold the mare back to him and allowed him to register her as Lady Andrew. The Duchess has always taken a real interest in the Hackney classes and in 1947 donated a challenge cup to be won three times by the same owner, and until recently always presented this herself. Lady Andrew had been a willful mare before George Daybell tamed her and had been sent to be schooled at Dick Midgeley's stables in Leeds. In 1947 she was entered for the coveted Hartington Cup. Miss Daybell takes up the story:

The day arrived... there was a wonderful entry of first class animals in both classes, but Dick was confident she could win. He was right – she did.

There were tears running down my face when I handed over the red rosette for the class. Then we had to wait for the championship in the afternoon and, what a thrill, Lady Andrew was pulled in as champion. When Lady Hartington came out to present the cup, she was so excited that she threw her arms round the mare's neck. Then Dick handed over the reins to my father to drive a lap of honour and I couldn't see a thing for tears.

Lady Andrew went on to win for the next three years and the Hartington Cup became theirs. It stood in the Daybell house for more than 30 years until the year Mary Daybell was president, when she gave it back to the society to be awarded in the future as the George Daybell trophy. In 1951, when Lady Andrew had retired, Miss Daybell had the honour of leading her with foal at foot at the show. The foal, Wyebank Magic, later won the Hartington Cup at Bakewell.

When George Daybell became too infirm to steward his daughter took over the responsibility, with help from Andrew Wain, his father Arnold, and later from Val and Brian Cooke. In 1999 she handed over the job completely to Andrew, Val and Brian.

Mary Daybell has some rich memories of her association with the show. In 1946 the secretary Jack Adams asked her to sew some roller towels for the ladies' toilets as well as stewarding. She remembers him as 'a lovely chap – but', she says 'you never spoke to him on show day because he used to get so worked up!'

The family lived at Wyebank Farm, Ashford in the Water, and every year until her father retired Mary used to help her mother to lay up the extended kitchen table and prepare a celebration meal for any Hackney members and friends who came back after the show:

Sometimes we used to have 30 or 40 people. I remember one year plaiting three horses' manes, helping my mother to lay the table, dashing to the show and stewarding the classes, then dashing back and feeding all these people with a cold buffet or high tea and what a party we had that first year we won the Hartington Cup.

One very wet day Mary got stuck in the mud after a wagon had churned up the field outside the pigeon and poultry area. Her boots were stuck fast and she had to be rescued by the Forces cadets, much to their amusement. She was revived by a cup of tea from Frank Clarke's wife in the pigeon and poultry tent.

Her father and Eddie Caudwell were among the first honorary life members. She and Sandy Caudwell now have the honour, but their badges – unlike their fathers' – were not made by Garrard, the royal jewellers. She has her father's on a ribbon, in a display case on her wall.

When she was president in 1981 friends came from Canada and Buxton Soroptimists, of which she was a founder member, gave the Mary Daybell Trophy for the Concourse d'Elegance and fielded a hospitality tent on both days; the profit from this provided a permanent seat in the Bath Gardens at Bakewell. On the show's second day it poured – half filling the Shires' big rosebowl with water, so she gave the winning horse a drink out of it during presentation of the trophies in the Grand Parade!

In 1996 Miss Daybell celebrated her 50th year as steward with a surprise presentation by the Duchess of Devonshire of a lovely china plate from the horse committee and flowers from her exhibitors, while the centre-ring PA system played Cliff Richard singing 'Congratulations'.

Her one big regret is that her spirit of adventure was thwarted. She managed a helicopter ride over the showground on the one and only occasion it was on offer, but she always wanted to go up in a hot-air balloon:

I thought I had secured the chance at the show when I was 70, until I discovered it involved having to climb into the basket, which I couldn't do. It was

a disappointment. I've never been up in a hot-air balloon and I shan't get the chance now, because I couldn't get in.

Joe Carson was just eight when he attended his first show – it was 4 August 1914 and the world was holding its breath and waiting for war:

My older brother was showing a young horse, a Shire colt, but we didn't stay long in Bakewell that day.

We had a driving mare, a cross-bred Hackney mare called Fanny. She was not only an exceptional animal, she was a family pet. When motor cars came out, she wanted to pass them and she often did. She had taken us to Bakewell that day and we had left her in the Rutland yard.

At the time the military were commandeering horses and had already looked around our farm. They'd fetched the mare out the stables twice and put her back again, but they were in Bakewell that day giving £50 for horses. My father thought we'd better get her out of the way, so we left early and came home. It was a successful rescue; Fanny never went to war.

When the show resumed after the war it became a regular family day out for the Carsons who farmed at Middleton-by-Youlgrave. Joe went on to become a member of the general committee in 1931, he was a sheep steward in the 1930s and a cattle steward after the Second World War. He served on both the livestock and finance committees, but still found time to compete in the show – his oats and cabbages won several prizes in the 1930s and he also received Highly Commended awards for mare and foal and Shorthorn heifer.

When Joe became president in 1967, he was only the second farmer to hold the honour in modern times. His presidential year was memorable for two reasons. The Young Farmers' Clubs presented their

Prime Minister Harold MacMillan (centre) with show director Matthew Longson (left), Joe Carson (right) and the Duke and Duchess of Devonshire behind. (McC)

famous cavalcade and there was a spectacular thunderstorm:

The lightening over Ballcross Plantation lit up the sky and a few days later I received a letter from Mr R.W.P. Cockerton, who had been president ten years earlier, congratulating me on such a wonderful display of fireworks.

Joe Carson was later made an honorary life member.

John Smallman took over as show director from Matthew Longson in 1975, after serving as assistant director for a number of years. A local land agent and chartered surveyor, he had lived in the town since 1954, when he came to work for a firm of auctioneers. Ten years later he set up his own business in Bakewell and opened another office in Matlock in 1966. His fascination for agricultural shows began when he was a small boy in Wales and used to take part in the showjumping. As a young man he got involved with the organisation and it was his job to hand the rosettes to the president at a time when such legendary names as Pat Smythe and Harry Llewellyn were competing. Showjumping remained his passion and he used to go around all the shows with his daughter Arabella who, at the time, jumped three horses.

It was under John Smallman's leadership that it was finally decided to make Bakewell a two-day show. One of the other highlights of his tenure was when he gave evidence at the public enquiry into plans to drive a massive trunk road through the 42-acre showground. He argued that it would have effectively split in half what he described as 'the nicest show setting in the United Kingdom'. Fortunately the plans were dropped.

He was president in 1982 when attractions included a fashion extravaganza and the appearance of 007's famous Saab turbo jet car. To mark his presidency he presented a new and very personal trophy. It belonged to his grandfather, an enthusiastic pigeon fancier who had won it with one of his birds in a top pigeon 'derby'. The refurbished trophy was to be awarded in a major showjumping event each year. He said at the time: 'I think my grandfather would have been thrilled to bits to hear what has happened to his cup.'

Brian Bakel has been show director since 1991, when he took over the reins on the retirement of John Smallman. He was in sole charge until the society become incorporated and created a joint directorship, and at the time of writing he shares the job with Richard Morten and Geoffrey Crawford. A softly-spoken Scotsman who was born and bred in Edinburgh, Brian Bakel's background is in farming and it was farming which brought him to Derbyshire in the first place. After studying agriculture at university he embarked on a successful career as a farm manager working in Oxfordshire and Kent, before he landed the job as farm manager at Chatsworth in 1963. Not surprisingly, given the Devonshires'

passion for the Bakewell Show, he became involved in various capacities including centre-ring steward and later as assistant director for 17 years – a job which brought with it a certain amount of trouble-shooting. It was his task to sort out the problems which occurred before and during the show. He was at the forefront of negotiations when Bakewell Agricultural Business Centre was built on the showground and held his breath as the development finished just days before the show was due to take place. As a result of all the work which he and joint director Richard Morten put in over the previous two years they were made honorary life patrons – the only such award that has ever been made. In 2001 he spearheaded the decision to go ahead with Bakewell Show when other events were cancelling due to foot and mouth. When he took over he said he was looking forward to the challenge – and the job has certainly lived up to that.

One of Brian's hobbies is sheep judging and he is a national judge for the Jacob Sheep Society which takes him to shows all over the country. He has judged at the Royal Show and the Royal Highland Show. He was president of Bakewell Show in 1987.

Geoffrey Crawford came to be part of Bakewell Show in the early 1990s, almost by default. He had retired from his job as finance director and company secretary of Chesterfield Tube Company Ltd (part of Steel TI) and was contemplating taking it easy when he was approached by Brian Nightingale, a tireless worker at the show:

He told me the show desperately needed a treasurer. I protested that I had retired, but nevertheless found myself talking to the committee. Edwin Mosley asked me why I wanted the job. I thought about it and I reckoned I had thoroughly enjoyed coming to the show over the years and now was the time to give something back.

Geoffrey Crawford can't have realised then that he would oversee two of the most significant developments in the show's history. The show committee wanted the office to be brought up to date so Geoffrey set about the task and within two years had computerised both accounts and administration. It was then decided that the society would become a company limited by guarantee. When he asked who was going to oversee the task he was told they hoped he would. So Geoffrey's next job was to set up the limited company, following which he was made a director along with Richard Morten and Brian Bakel. After that it was time to modernise the computer system... and all this while he was carrying out normal treasurer's duties such as looking after the show's finances, balancing tickets against gate receipts and paying out prizes at show time. He recalls:

I have overseen two major changes both of which underline the fact that this is no longer a farmers' club, it's big business. Until the year of foot and mouth disease we had made a profit. That year we knew we were going to make a loss and planned for it. But the bad weather in 2002 was something no-one could plan for, and the costs were out of everyone's control.

Geoffrey, helped by assistant treasurer Leonard Twigg, now not only oversees the show's financial dealings, but ensures that all the main show contracts are in place.

Robin and Wendy Rhodes are show people largely thanks to her father Eric Hague. He ran an office equipment company in Doncaster, but was, says Wendy, always a frustrated farmer. Eric and his wife Marjorie were patrons, so the family came to the show every year, staying in their caravan at Calver until they moved to the area in 1967. Eric's interest was soon picked up by Lt-Col Harry Wise from Ashford, president in 1963, and before he knew it he was involved in the show as chairman of car parks, entrances and, in those days, the grandstand. Meanwhile Marjorie did her bit in the first-aid tent.

Eric was due to be president in 1984, but sadly died in January before he could take office. It was as a result of his death, which left them without a successor, that the society changed the rules and now always elects a vice-president and a president elect.

Robin had helped his father-in-law a few times and he was approached to join the show committee. At first he declined, but later was persuaded to become chairman of car parks, entrances and now security. Some years later Wendy was asked by Sandy Caudwell if she would like to become a cattle steward. After discovering that this involved being near cows she decided she would rather steward in food and farming. She later went on the committee, becoming chairman in 2000. Two years later Robin was made president – a bitter-sweet moment for Wendy. She recalls:

When my father was due to be president I remember sitting in the grandstand with my mother joking that she should watch carefully to see what to do when the huge Charolais bull was in the centre ring because she would be doing it the following year. Of course it didn't happen. But some time later mother told me that father had planned that when the bull came into the ring he was going to announce that his daughter would present that particular trophy. Little did I realise that I really would do it one day as the wife of the president.

Robin's memories are mostly of organising the towing of mud-bound vehicles on and off the showground following bad weather – and of the fantastic relationship he built up with the veterans of Chesterfield Parachute Regiment Association who looked after security for five years before handing over to the Royal Signals. But he also remembers the time when a trade-stand holder was complaining that he was having to wait while the stockmen brought cattle on to the ground. He told Robin: 'I've got items worth £500 each in my van.' Robin told him: 'Well that cattle truck which has just gone past contains a bull which has just been brought over from Canada that's worth £20,000.' No contest. On another occasion he watched in admiration as a 20-something young woman backed a 42-ton cattle truck 30 or 40 yards into the stock overflow field, shortly before a well-known showjumper argued that he couldn't possibly do the same thing – which of course he could, and did to save face.

Lady Winifred Hilton, widow of the late Sir Peter Hilton, was an enthusiastic supporter of the show and a great favourite with show-goers in her spectacularly pretty hats, some of which she admitted were 50 years old. One hat in particular was favoured by a horse in the centre ring the year her husband Peter was president. As Lady Winifred waited patiently to present the cups the horse decided to have a nibble at the exotic creation.

President herself in 1998, Lady Winifred was a very popular choice, particularly with the ex-Service personnel whom she would greet personally. She had served in the Women's Auxiliary Airforce and had a lot of respect for the old soldiers. When she toured the showground it took joint director Brian Bakel twice as long because she insisted on stopping and talking to everyone she knew – and she knew a lot of people! Of her presidency she said:

It was the most wonderful privilege and honour and I shall remember everyone's kindness with great gratitude. My family has always lived in Derbyshire and I was born at Scotland House near Tansley. As a child my parents always brought me to Bakewell Show every year which I so looked forward to.

Since the age of five until the present day I never missed attending except during the war years when I was in the WAAF.

I have always loved Bakewell Show and been so very proud of its achievement in becoming one of the largest one-day shows in the country. My great love is the Shire horses which we used at our Scotland Nurseries for ploughing and pulling the heavy drays to deliver the trees, I grew up with them and around them and things were never the same when we turned to tractors.

When **Andrew Derbyshire** went into the family nursery business he knew it would be hard work, but he also knew there would be spin-off pleasures – including Bakewell Show.

The show had been part of his life since childhood. His father used to go and landscape around all the banks on the site and when Andrew, his brother Richard and sister Anthea were old enough they went along too, supposedly to help:

It was a real thrill preparing for the show and watching everybody hard at work. We'd all help until we lost interest and then we'd wander off to see what we could find. There was always a wonderful display of tractors and Richard was besotted by them. One year when it was time to go home, he was nowhere to be see. Then they found him helping to paint the wheels of one of his beloved tractors.

Anthea was fascinated by the show stand put on by Mills of Bakewell. They used to have a four-foot-high leather boot as part of their display. I loved everything, but my favourite was going round on the horse-drawn cart filling up the water jump in the main ring.

People with trade stands seemed to spend a lot more time preparing in those days. Today they seem to arrive after nine on the day before the show and they are gone again by early evening on the Thursday.

I remember the excitement of the first combine harvester which came to the show from Nottingham. Even in those days farmers didn't travel around a lot and the show was one of the few opportunities they had to see the new machinery and equipment.

It was also an opportunity for them to get something back from the feed merchants they used all year. On show days you'd see all the farmers in their best suits in the hospitality tents by the ringside tucking into a solid lunch provided by the feed merchants. Now I think they are lucky to get a cup of tea.

Andrew Derbyshire, president in 1994, is closely associated with the show's horse committee.

Jack Armitage was president in 1983, exactly 50 years after his father Cecil had the honour. He first came to the show in 1921 when he came third in the children's riding class. His mount Dobbin was not exactly a show pony – it used to pull his mother's trap from Great Longstone to Bakewell – but was good enough to win young Jack 7s.6d. which he spent buying 'a very good camera'. He entered several more times, but without the same success. And he missed out on his dad's presidential year too: 'Although it was the time of the depression, the family mill at Salford was working six days a week and I had to be there.'

Betty Haller who served on the horticulture committee for 40 years until her retirement in 1998 made her mark by easing tensions between Bakewell's flower arrangers and horticulturalists. A founder member of both Bakewell and Holmesfield flower clubs, she helped set up other groups in the area at a time when flower arranging started to be taken up by people other than those who lived in big houses.

In 1958 her mother, who lived near the showground, sold some land to the society and when the show secretary came to finalise arrangements he

President Jack Armitage presenting prizes to the trade stand winners. (CU)

recognised Betty as the winner of Best in Show the previous year. He asked her to join the horticulture committee and so began four decades of involvement.

In those days snobbery was a bit of a problem among the floral exhibitors, the exclusive preserve of people like the gardeners from the big houses doing 'four corners and a middle for the table'. Betty recalls:

They didn't really like the flower arrangers, they thought we were just silly women who bought flowers and didn't grow them. This was an attitude that I had to break down.

For a long time we were the also-rans and we didn't matter very much. One man was very anti and one day, while I was judging a small show, he was my steward. I down-pointed one exhibit because it was wilting... and he suggested I didn't know much about flowers, so I told him I'd take him on!

Betty challenged him to name as many of the flowers as he could:

He was completely stumped! He was a wonderful grower of one type of flower and had won prizes all over the place. But he didn't know the others by their Latin names like I did. He backed down and after that gave me a great deal of respect and help. It was really a battle of knowledge, but it's something we've all had to work at. Even at Chelsea there's this attitude.

Betty Haller went on to become a national judge for the National Association of Flower Arranging Societies (NAFAS) – for which she was required to know all the Latin names. She was later honoured with life membership of the society.

Frank Clarke has been exhibiting poultry since he was a schoolboy – and in 2005 the 'schoolboy' will

become show president. Frank has been involved in the organisation for around 30 years and chairman of the small livestock committee for more than 20 years. In that time he has seen the pigeons, poultry and rabbit section doubled to almost 800 entries. Under his guidance the show earned Regional Championship status from the National Poultry Club in the 1980s and has maintained the annual award ever since.

Dorrie Patterson took over as chairman of the dog section in the 1970s when the long-serving Frank Twiggs retired, and since then she has seen it grow into one of the largest and most well-respected open dog shows in the North of England, with more than 2,000 dogs representing at least 92 breeds travelling to Bakewell from all over the British Isles and some from Europe. Dorrie ensures that everything runs smoothly, a task which can be very challenging, but she and her committee always meet the challenge.

In 2001 Bakewell Show was awarded the Golden Bone award which is given to the best run and organised open show in the country. This was an honour for the dog show people and they are particularly proud of winning the award as it was nominated and voted for by the dog-showing exhibitors: 'Everyone works very hard encouraging dog owners to come here and we have a lot of very willing volunteers – we couldn't manage without them.' One of those volunteers is Dorrie's own husband Bill who also serves on the dog section as show manager. But the family connection with Bakewell Show doesn't end there – their daughter Julia is chairman of the trade-stand committee and Dorrie is due to be president of the show in 2004.

Frank Clarke, chairman of the pigeon and poultry section, shows the Duchess of Rutland a prizewinning bird. (CU)

Left: *The late Ted Brownhill, show secretary from 1976–94.*

Three former presidents (left to right): Brian Bakel, Edwin Mosley and Sandy Caudwell. (CU)

❧ Nine ❧

Money and Sponsorship

On a good day, when the sun is shining and the showground is full of visitors, it is difficult to believe that Bakewell Show could ever face financial problems. But in 2003 it costs in excess of one-third of a million pounds to stage the show and the figure is rising each year. It takes only two consecutive years of poor attendance for whatever reason for the situation to become grave, and the sinking fund to sink without trace. And as history illustrates only too clearly money and sponsorship have always been a problem.

Even as early as 1834 the frail and ageing father of the society, Wootten Thomas, was lamenting the fact that so many members were in arrears with their subs – and that was at a time when the finances were relatively healthy. Indeed prizes at the early shows seemed quite generous with three guineas for the best bull, dairy cow or draught horse, two guineas for other first-prize winners and one guinea for second.

Sponsors, in both cash and kind, and donors are the lifeblood of the society, but, despite the show being a superb commercial platform, it is becoming increasingly difficult to attract financial support. Probably the earliest sponsor was the Board of Agriculture which in 1821 awarded a silver vase worth 30 guineas to the best cultivated farm in the society's area. Undoubtedly other trophies were forthcoming, but the next recorded donation was more than 30 years later when the president Sir Joseph Paxton gave two silver trophies, one worth £5 and one worth £10, for the best cultivated farms of over 50 and over 125 acres.

President Mr E.A. Hoyle's offer to present a silver cup for a farming competition at the end of his term of office in 1923 caused organisers a few problems because it was felt that farming in North Derbyshire varied so much that it would be very difficult to be fair. They suggested a herd competition instead and Mr Hoyle agreed that rather than a silver cup he would give £25. The show did end up with its cup though. The judge, Shorthorn breeder Mr H.C. Holm of Carlton Curlieu, Leicester, said that he would forgo his expenses if the society bought a silver cup to be awarded to the owner of the best herd in the two classes.

By 1929 the society, now 60 years old, owned a total of 14 silver trophies. How the show was financed in those days is not entirely clear – but gate receipts in 1877 amounted to a 'record' £67, suggesting that visitors were not relied upon, although they were to play an increasingly important role. In 1892 a jubilant *Derbyshire Times* applauded a Mr Smith for his record gate-takings: 'Well done Mr Smith that you should take £290 at the gate, the largest haul ever is something to be proud of.' And the following year when 3,000 people came to the show, gate receipts went up to £470.

One of the main problems facing organisers was the fact that ever-increasing costs and rising prize money left no margin for setting up a contingency fund and when, as happened in 1904, the show was a washout there was nothing to fall back on. More lean years were to follow and the situation became worse with just £50 in the show's account following the 1909 show. After that the Dukes of Devonshire and Rutland agreed to underwrite the losses.

One way of raising money to help fund the show catalogue was to sell advertising space for products obviously aligned to an agricultural show... and one or two for items which were less obvious. The Baker Unit henhouse was advertised one year – a five-star affair with flush fitting door, bob hole, large mash box and nest box. 'At just £13 per house with carriage paid, the poultry farmer just cannot help but obtain the maximum return on his capital,' the advert enthused. And then there was Spillers Osoko dog food, 'the paramount dog food which puts that little extra into a dog which catches the judges' eye.' It is not recorded how much Spillers paid the show, but the name appeared at the top of every page in the catalogue with Winalot eventually replacing Osoko.

William Britt and Sons' glass milk bottles personalised with enamel or sandblasting, Silcocks' pig-rearing meal and the Samson safety bull tether from the Sheffield Wire Rope Company were all obvious contenders for farming folk. But where does 'Ask to see a demonstration of the new Hoover vacuum cleaner' fit in with H. Broughton and Sons, gents outfitters? And why was J.W. Stewart and Co. advertising ladies swimwear from 1s.6d.?

By 1935 it was costing £5,800 to stage the show, but careful investment meant that organisers had built up a buffer to cope with any losses they might face. After the war, in the golden years of record attendance, they might have been forgiven for thinking they were safe, but an ill-judged decision to stage the show on a Saturday saw numbers fall dramatically and big losses.

NatWest Bank has been a staunch supporter of Bakewell Show for a number of years. (CU)

Above: *Promoting the show on television.* (McC)

Above: *Award-winning ice-cream manufacturer Bruno Frederick hands over the Shire horse trophy to F. Robinson Ltd. The company is a regular sponsor of the show.* (CU)

Above: *Bakewell Show promoting itself at Chatsworth Game Fair in 1975.*

Right: *How the sponsorship worked with improved signage and, in the distance, the pagodas for the band.*

Ann Lamb, wife of the Chairman and Chief Executive of the Gordon Lamb Group, Richard Lamb, presents a horse brass to the winner of the vintage car section watched by president Andrew Derbyshire.

In 1972 they were back in debt and forced to issue a public plea for donations after suffering a £4,000 shortfall – but again they survived.

Weather conditions in 1979 were atrocious and, despite sponsors giving away more than £8,000 as prize money for various events and showjumping sponsors combining to increase their prize money to £800, the show just failed to break even, leading the show director John Smallman to tell the annual meeting:

It is essential that we try to balance our budget for each show and remember that reserves are vital if the show is to continue successfully and the committee has this in mind when asking for increases in subscriptions and patrons' fees from 1980.

However, he didn't exactly follow his own advice when he was president two years later. He had visited Hickstead the previous year and, being a Welshman, had booked the Band of the Welsh Guards to appear at his presidential show – without actually working out how they were going to pay for them. As it turned out he need not have worried because an appeal for funds attracted donations of between £50 and £500 enabling the visit to go ahead.

He later paid an effusive tribute to local firms who, he said, formed the backbone of many bids to attract big names to Bakewell Show, singling out one particular West Derbyshire businessman who came to the rescue when 'an opportunity arose which was too good to miss.'

'Ever-increasing costs mean that we are always on the lookout for more sponsors. Those who have stood by us and the one-off sponsors are greatly appreciated', noted John Smallman. But even with the extra donations the show sailed very close to the financial wind that year: the *Star* reported a surplus of just £278 due to 'an alarming increase in the cost of staging the show'. The situation was increasingly serious. Costs had risen from a reported £21,000 in 1964 to a staggering £100,000 in 1983 and organisers launched an urgent appeal for more sponsors. At the time ticket prices accounted for nearly half the show's income and money from trade stands, car parking, grandstand tickets and class entry fees together with sponsorship and donations made up the rest. It didn't take much to work out that any drop in attendance would have a wide-reaching effect on the show. And what if there were expenses which hadn't been budgeted for – as happened in 1987? The show had made a profit of more than £10,000, when organisers suddenly found themselves with a bill for £11,500 for laying underground electricity cables on the showground. The shortfall was paid for by a rise in ticket prices – but it could only be a modest rise, because too much of an increase would drive people away.

Somehow they continued to balance the books and survive, even the disastrous £14,000 loss of 1990. Then in 1993 a deal was struck which has meant that, with the exception of the planned losses during the last foot-and-mouth outbreak and the uncontrollable deficit in 2002, the show has become solvent again.

The Chesterfield-based Gordon Lamb Group, celebrating its 40th anniversary, stepped in with a

57

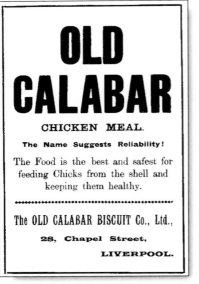

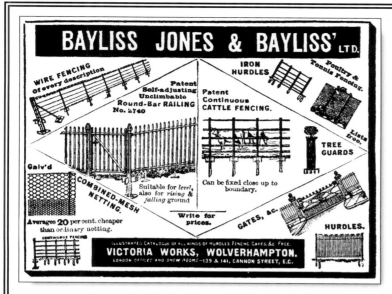

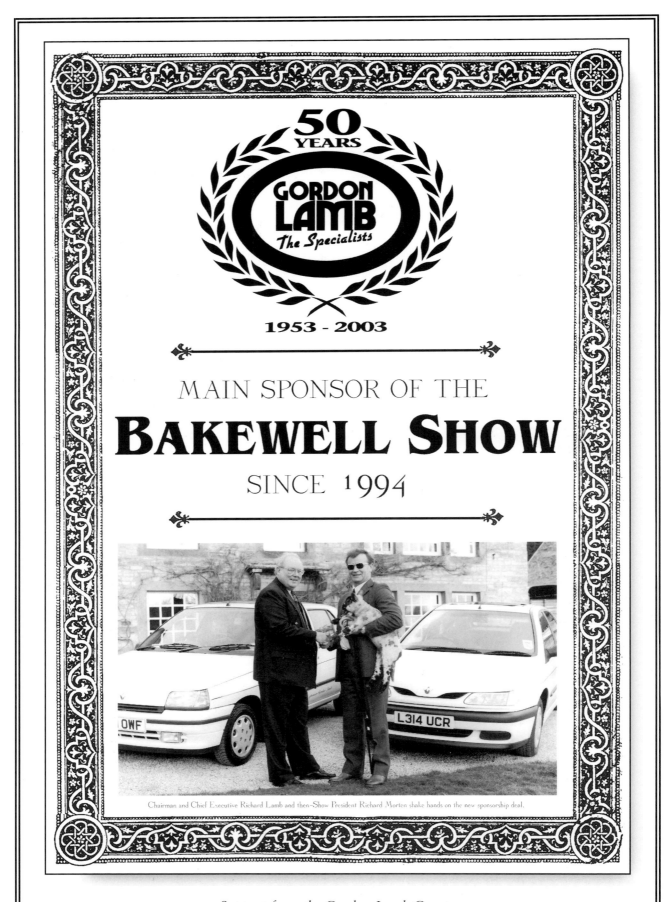

Chairman and Chief Executive Richard Lamb and then-Show President Richard Morten shake hands on the new sponsorship deal.

Support from the Gordon Lamb Group.

61

three-year deal worth in excess of £75,000. It has proved so mutually beneficial that it is now an open-ended agreement. Part of the deal was a smart new logo incorporating the main sponsor's name which is used in all Gordon Lamb advertising in the weeks before the show, helping to raise the profile of the event and keep it in the public eye. Having Bakewell Show so closely associated with a motor dealership, covering seven different franchises, was in danger of attracting a lot of criticism, but managing director Richard Lamb was adamant that his approach would be softly-softly with the emphasis on enhancing areas of need rather than ramming home a corporate message. An unashamed lover of Bakewell Show and a life patron for a number of years, he said at the time:

I deem myself very fortunate to be sponsoring the show. It gives me the opportunity to put something back into a community which has given me so much pleasure in the past.

For show director Brian Bakel it was something of a relief to have attracted such high-profile sponsorship as the show struggled to survive in an increasingly commercial environment. As he said at the time:

The plain fact is that we can no longer meet our costs from turnstyle receipts alone. We are the largest tented show in the country with a canvas bill of £80,000. Judging and policing accounts for a further £35,000, prize money is in excess of £20,000 and the wage bill for permanent staff is £40,000.

Of course we have had sponsors before, whether in a small way, sponsoring one class, or on a larger scale, sponsoring a whole section, we value their continued support – but the Gordon Lamb deal takes us into a completely new area so we are grateful for the opportunities it will give us.

The biggest PR exercise organisers faced, however, was to persuade the army of volunteers on whom the show relies so heavily that the deal would benefit them. But the new staging, new signage and presti-gious new trophies which began to appear soon had the majority agreeing it was a good thing. Integrating the company into the show was a fine balancing act as Gordon Lamb's then marketing director Tony Lynn underlined:

It would be so easy to spoil something with such a great tradition. But Bakewell Show has evolved over many decades and to change it would be sacri-lege. The reason it works is that it has the help of hundreds of volunteers. We didn't want to upset that balance or those volunteers or for them to feel in any way that it was not their show any more.

We have also had to think about other sponsors, whether it is the person who supplies the straw for

the goats free of charge or the company which presents a major trophy, we didn't want them to feel that we have come crashing in and taken over.

Indeed the relationship has worked well and the show's other sponsors are comfortable with the devel-opment. Among big contributors are NatWest and the Royal Bank of Scotland which sponsor livestock, and Aggregate Industries which makes a contribution towards the Horse of the Year Show qualifiers.

During the horticulture section's centenary, Citroen UK stepped in with £3,000 to fund a special marquee for demonstrations and a Gardeners' Question Time feature. And up to 2002 the Sheffield-based Westside Magazine Group made a cash donation and produced the official programme and catalogue for the show. That mantle has been taken over by Sheffield Newspapers and now includes a substantial amount of advertising as well.

There is also a lot of small sponsorship of indi-vidual classes and simple donations from people wanting to help the show. And when specific items are needed such as a fitted kitchen and cooker in a food and farming demonstration theatre, local companies usually come up trumps in exchange for a trade-stand space and some advertising.

With around 50,000 people visiting the show each year, it is the perfect vehicle for a variety of businesses to get their message across and organisers work tire-lessly to explore new avenues for help. But they are adamant that sponsorship is a two-way deal, which is why donation-related sponsorship packages have been introduced to include free entry tickets and advertising both in the show publications and with banners on the showground.

There have been other attempts to raise funds to keep the show afloat by renting out the showground out of show time for numerous activities such as car-boot sales, caravan rallies and flower festivals. A special events and fund-raising committee was set up and stalwarts Sandy Caudwell and Wendy Rhodes organised a variety of money-spinners including concerts and quizzes. The food and farming committee arranged fashion shows and lunches to try to help meet their costs and other sections make an effort too.

Unfortunately the general council cannot agree to every request; some events such as the steam-engine rally proposed by one organisation simply create too much damage for the showground to recover.

But, as costs continue to rise, organisers are acutely aware that, even with the Gordon Lamb deal, they must continue to be good housekeepers, keeping costs down and putting on a show which will attract not only new support but a new generation of visitors too. Because if Bakewell Show is to thrive in the twenty-first century it must have a firm financial foundation, and that means more members, more sponsors and more people through the gate at show time.

Ten

The Organisation

The morning after the show the office is still awash with adrenaline, there's bucks fizz and homemade cake and lots of laughter as organisers swap stories about what has happened to them over the past two days. The phone continues to ring; a few disgruntled punters and a sprinkling of people wanting to know what time the show opens, but they're too late. Then at around midday it stops as the bubble bursts and reality hits – it's all over for another year. The workers go home tired and deflated.

For the committee chairmen it is time for a breather, but for the office staff it is back to work on Monday morning for a massive clearing-up session. As the last trade stand leaves on the Thursday evening the striking of tents begins. Some of the larger marquees are left to host extra out-of-show functions. Traditionally the local Young Farmers stage a disco on the Thursday and the Old Mannerians Rugby Club a disco on the Friday. And for the past couple of years a local auctioneer has held a house-clearance sale in the horticultural tent over the weekend. But the important thing is to get enough of the showground cleared to hand back the land to the council for car parking on the Monday.

Back in the office the girls have the mammoth job of collating the results, checking them and sorting out any queries with the committee chairmen or duty stewards ready for the de-briefing session which always takes place a week after the show. The de-brief is a mix of business meeting and social occasion. Each committee chairman gives a report highlighting the good aspects as well as anything which went wrong with suggestions of how it could be rectified for the following year. Even in the years when there have been problems the majority of reports have been very positive and good-humoured and the chairmen very buoyant about their section's success.

The office staff continue to be busy throughout August writing to all of the committee members,

Early television coverage

sponsors, contractors and judges thanking them and paying outstanding expenses and bills. By the end of the month all the prize money will have been paid and any complaints dealt with. Organisers take complaints very seriously. Any member of the public whose problem cannot be dealt with on show days is invited to fill in a special form which is then handed to the committee chairman responsible. If a refund is deemed necessary it will be sent out and if there is an overwhelming number of complaints about one particular aspect – as there was with uncomfortable grandstand seats one year – that will be noted to be changed for the following show.

By September the office is back to its 'regulars' – show manager, currently Clare Fletcher, two full-time staff and assistant treasurer Leonard Twigg. Incredibly these are the only organisers on the payroll – everyone else, including the directors, management committee, council members, committee members, stewards and general helpers are volunteers. It is time to start doing the trade schedules for the following year. All of the committees will meet over the next few weeks, but the trade-stand committee is one of the first because it is necessary to sort out electricity request forms and health and safety information in plenty of time. There are nine section committees – for food and farming; horticulture; pigeons, poultry and rabbits; horses; livestock; floral art; catering; car parking; and centre ring – as well as the finance committee and the main council. When the committees hold their first meeting after the show they have an inquest into their performance and then set about planning for the following year, which starts with the election of a new chairman.

Over the coming weeks the committees will plan the new schedules, decide who they want to be judges and whether or not they want to add any new classes. Judges are invited as far in advance as possible – in the case of the horse classes it can be up to four years ahead – because the popular ones are snapped up early.

Everything is brought together in draft... and then the whole process stops until November when the finance committee meets. This meeting is pivotal to the whole show – it is when anything that will cost money is either agreed or rejected. By then the finance committee will know whether the previous show has been a success or otherwise and be able to allocate funds accordingly. But even after that meeting the schedules cannot go to the printers because everything decided at the finance committee has to be ratified by the general council.

By December the horticultural trade schedules have been sent out to potential exhibitors followed by general trade stand and food and farming brochures in January.

The new year begins with a flurry of activity as the show manager continues to lay the foundations for that year's event. Existing sponsors are contacted and asked if they will help the show again and potential new ones are courted for their support. The WI schedules are compiled and sent out along with letters to visitors who book grandstand seats each year asking if they want to book them again.

The annual report is prepared with the audited accounts and the life members and patrons list updated. The show notes – prepared by Robin Rhodes, in charge of car parks and president in 2002 – are put together. They will be sent out along with notices of other events such as the regular car-boot sales, the twice-yearly flower festival held on the showground and the local farmers' markets.

It is important that the competitive horticulture schedules go out in February because many of the entrants grow their flowers and vegetables according to the classes. The rest of the schedules will go out in March and April after the different affiliations have been checked and brought up to date. In the case of the livestock, horses and rabbits this means contacting all the different breed societies to make sure the classes comply with their rules.

March also sees a meeting with Derbyshire police to check the level of policing which is required. Normally the show pays for a sergeant and six constables to patrol the showground – a figure supplemented by specials and Bakewell bobbies on their regular beat. By April the momentum is building up – the new president, vice-president and president-elect are installed, the council and auditors elected and life memberships are awarded to outstanding show supporters.

The office will contact stewards asking for their help and committees will be asked what furniture they need so that it can be ordered. It is also time to sort out the number of tickets and rosettes which will be needed. Getting the tickets right is crucial to the success of the show. Bus companies, tourist information centres and local shops and offices, who sell them on a commission basis, need to be contacted for their requirements and organisers have to estimate how many others will be needed.

Over the last decade the allocation of tickets has become far more professional with each ticket being numbered so that it can be tracked, resulting in a much tighter operation and less margin for error. The introduction of the 'Open for Business' exhibition during the foot-and-mouth crisis year was such a success that it is now a regular feature, creating an extra job for office staff. Space is limited, but small businesses which supported the exhibition the previous year are invited again and spare trade stands are allocated to other applicants.

With just 12 weeks to go organisers meet with the main contractors. The overall contracts – some for just a year and others, including tentage and catering, for three years – will have been negotiated by the directors the previous autumn. This meeting is called to finalise arrangements. It is also necessary to meet with the show's main sponsor motor dealer Gordon Lamb to check out their space requirements.

Other meetings take place: with the St John Ambulance to agree first-aid coverage; with Derbyshire Dales District Council and Bakewell Agricultural Business Centre to agree the washing down of the Cattle Market, the emptying of the slurry tanks, groundwork – and the all-important dates when the show can take over the site; and with the local Job Centre.

Because contractors and trade stand holders prefer to use local labour during show time organisers work in conjunction with the Job Centre to help find it. Together they plan a flier which they send out suggesting that if they 'order' particular skills early, their needs are likely to be met.

By now the regular staff have been joined by the show team who are brought in to help as the pace hots up. In past years it has been girls from the local Lady Manners School – ideally one who has been the previous year and one new girl prepared to come the following year as well. But often they enjoy the work so much that some of them continue to come in their holidays from university.

Adverts for the show will already have appeared in trade and tourism publications earlier in the year, but in June the pre-publicity begins with 'trailer' articles and interviews. Notification of the press conference two weeks before the show are sent out, awakening media interest, and the press pack is prepared, giving details of the attractions and the key people involved in the organisation.

On the admin side entries are beginning to close for the different sections and each has to be entered on the computer, allocated a number, and all the relevant tickets and passes have to be sent out. This is a time-consuming exercise because it is necessary to check that if one animal is entered in two classes it can realistically get from one place to another in time.

Attention also turns to the president in June. Traditionally the president's dinner is held on Tuesday night after the opening ceremony when the president's own guests are invited, together with committee chairmen and others, such as sponsors, who are important to the show. On show days there are two presidential lunches – and the office is responsible for organising invitations to these too.

(CU)

Meanwhile the showground plan has been finalised and trade-stand space allocated, working closely with the show electrician and the plumber to make sure that services are where they are needed. Plumber Mick Ford *(above)* has been working at the show for years. He moved to Provence in France some time ago but still makes the pilgrimage to Bakewell each summer because he enjoys the event so much. Apart from the necessary standpipes it is his job to ensure that the toilets and showers are adequate for the armies of people who stay on the showground for up to a week. In early July showground co-ordinator Mike Patterson and his team of four lads move on to the showground to start preparing for the influx of animals, traders and businesses. They mark out the trade stands both on the showground and in marquees such as food and farming, paint toilets and fences, cut grass, fill in any holes and generally make themselves useful fetching and carrying. Later they will be responsible for counting the furniture and making sure the different sections have what they ordered.

In the office the girls have taken the information needed for the catalogue from the database and sent it to the printers and also dispatched members' and patrons' packs.

With just two weeks to go the countdown has begun and from here on the girls in the office will work every day, often from 6a.m. to 10p.m. until the show is over. The press conference is held when representatives from the local and regional media gather to hear about the highlights of the forthcoming show. There are television and radio interviews with the directors and show manager and details of coverage are finalised.

Already on the showground there is evidence of the event – stacks of tent poles and piles of canvas wait to be erected and demountable fencing not needed during the show is removed and stored. On the Thursday before the big day the stewards' briefing is held – usually in the members' marquee – when the show director delivers a rallying call to all the volunteers and an entry update is given as a yardstick to the probable success of the show. Janet Bailey, in charge of health and safety on the site, outlines some of the would-be

dangers and reiterates the 'grid' system which is in place in case of emergencies. Because of its military links and animal rights activities, Bakewell Show is a potential terrorist target, so one of the more unusual talks is given by a Special Branch officer, who alerts stewards to look out for suspicious objects.

When the talking is over stewards for each section collect a specially-packed bag or basket containing all the necessary tickets, passes, rosettes and paperwork and drink a toast to the success of the following week.

By Friday the activity has become frenetic; committee chairman are on site making sure their staging is in place ready for the exhibits and the trade stands have begun to arrive. In the office the phone rings incessantly with queries from people wanting to know anything from prices and dates to whether there is any trade stand space left.

Janet Bailey, accompanied by a policeman, patrols the ground to check that health-and-safety regulations are being obeyed. These have become much more stringent in recent years following directives from Europe and it is vital that the show keeps abreast of them. A long-term weather forecast will have been studied and contingency plans put in place in case of bad weather with tractors standing by to pull vehicles on and off the showground in the event of a downpour.

Judging of the competitive cheese and meat products classes as well as the WI competitions takes place on the day before the show and in the office final arrangements are being made for the opening service that evening and for the president's dinner which follows. Traditionally the showground is open for visitors to see the finishing touches being put to the exhibits and trade stands are able to sell their wares. The girls stay late that night to answer last-minute queries.

Although the show doesn't officially open until 9a.m., volunteers and organisers are on the show-ground from around 6a.m. There's a wonderful air of anticipation and everyone is on a high – probably because anything which has not been done by then won't get done.

For the organisers the first day is more stressful than the second. It is then that most of the problems

Girls working in the show office. (CU)

67

occur and the girls in the office have to gather every ounce of their diplomacy to try to deal with them. Often it is simply down to visitors being stuck in a traffic jam or leaving their passes at home and having to pay again. But director Richard Morten and a police constable are stationed in the office throughout the day to make sure things don't get out of control. Show manager Clare Fletcher spends much of the day patrolling the show with another policeman. She takes time to build relationships with the trade stand holders and the visitors – that way if problems do arise they can be solved in a friendly way.

The girls in the office do manage to get out of the office during the show – having spent all that time organising the event, they want time to enjoy it free from tannoy announcements and radio telephones. They operate a flexible shift system so they all have some time off.

There is a round of television and radio interviews which joint directors Richard Morten and Brian Bakel (when he is not on official duties with the president) and show manager Clare Fletcher handle between them. At 6.30p.m. a debriefing of all the committee chairmen is called to find out if anything that has happened can be put right before the following day's show. If it can, it is, if not a mental note is made to address the problem for next year. Thursday proceeds in much the same way as Wednesday – only this time as the show draws to a close there is a determined effort by organisers to stop traders from leaving the showground before the show closes at 6p.m. as this can be very dangerous with thousands of visitors still walking around.

How does it all run so smoothly, with organisers staying sane? Show manager Clare Fletcher explains:

When the adrenaline starts pumping it's important that the team is in good spirits. Over the weeks we have built up a really good relationship – we need that bond because we put so much pressure on each other it would be very easy to fall out. Every year things happen, but every year it's the good things that you remember.

So the show closes and the morning after the office is still awash with that adrenaline...

Right: *Staging arriving on the showground ready to be erected.* (CU)

Below: *A week before the show the stewards gather for a briefing.* (CU)

Left: *The team for the 2002 show* (left to right) *Sarah Lee, Tracey Wilkins, show manager Clare Fletcher, Leyanne Beacham and Mary Gregory.* (CU)

Below: *The garden surrounding the office must look neat and tidy.* (CU)

Eleven

The Military Connection

There is no obvious correlation between a peace-loving rural pursuit like Bakewell Show and the military, but records show that the event does have a proud military connection. Over the years a number of high-ranking officers have served as president – from as early as 1829 when the honour fell to Major William Carleill of Longstone Hall, to more recent names, Captain Charles Waterhouse of Middleton Hall, Lt-Col Sir Ian Walker-Okeover of Osmaston Manor and Col Sir Peter Hilton of Alton Manor.

But it is the soldiers who have come to Bakewell from regiments all over the world who will go down in history for their breathtaking and colourful displays. And curiously it is also possible to trace the progress of world conflict through the show records by seeing who did and who did not manage to attend the show.

The First World War cast a shadow over the 1914 show. It was not just that the Army was requisitioning cattle trucks and horseboxes, and taking work horses to plough up spare grassland, nor that the Government cancelled all excursion trains, which meant visitors couldn't come by rail, but there were labour issues too. As farmers struggled to bring in the harvest before their workforces were called up, Bakewell Show was not their first priority. Nonetheless, the event went ahead, but was then suspended until 1920.

After the bloody conflict people wanted to have fun and during the interwar years many of the country's most distinguished regiments came and entertained – names like the 2nd Battalion Northumberland Fusiliers, the Royal Scots Greys, the Royal Inniskillin Dragoon Guards and the Royal Signals.

But the glory years came after the Second World War. In 1949 the Household Cavalry – the monarch's personal bodyguard set up by Charles II in 1661 – came to perform their famous musical ride. There was a fanfare by mounted trumpeters followed by regimental slow marches by the Life Guards and the Royal Horse Guards. It thrilled the crowd, but in particular one young lady, who was to go on and become show president. Mary Daybell recalls:

I remember the first time the Household Cavalry came to Bakewell Show. It was a glorious sunny day and the spectacle of seeing them in their uniforms with their breastplates shining was unforgettable. It was such a thrill – absolutely wonderful. They came by train and it cost £1,000 to bring them, which was a lot of money back then, and horses and men were posted on the ground.

Years later, when current joint director Brian Bakel was president, the son of show stalwart (and later president), Major Hugo Waterhouse, was commanding the Household Cavalry at the show. In a touching break from tradition, Major Waterhouse was invited to take the salute.

The 1953 Bakewell Show played host to the Massed Pipe Bands of the Brigade of Ghurkas, who had won so many hearts with their bravery during the war. The band, which paid a return visit in 1960, just weeks ahead of a state visit by the King of Nepal, was made up of around 100 men from six different battalions, representing the 250-strong band which regularly turned out for ceremonial occasions in Malaya. In 1955 it was the turn of the Massed Band of the Arab Legion, and while their music was welcomed with great enthusiasm, they managed to cause something of a headache for catering director William Noble. Traditionally workers, officers and bandsmen tuck into an early-morning farmers' breakfast of bacon and egg – but their religion prohibited the Transjordan musicians from eating the bacon. Still they did like English tea and, according to the catering director, 'drank lashings!'

The following year the Royal Corps of Signals gave a display supported by the Malaya Police Band, whose members had lived in primitive jungle villages before joining the force. Another exotic band was scheduled to appear at the 1957 show, but in the event the King's African Rifles and Corps of Drums were drowned out when the centre-ring entertainment was cancelled because of a severe thunderstorm. The Ugandan regiment, which only months before had been fighting a grim battle with Mau Mau terrorists in Kenya, had come to the show from the Royal Tournament.

The 1964 show brought the Royal Tank Regiment's Cambrian, Alamein and Rhine battalions together for the first time. The Band of the Fiji Military Forces at the 1965 show was something of a culture shock to the more sedate show-goers. The 60 warriors from the romantic island of Sura were

Above: *The Band of the Royal Regiment of Fusiliers performed in 1983.*

Left: *A military band entertains.*

Below: *The Band of the Yorkshire Volunteers – always popular with today's show crowd.*

Above: *The band of the Arab Legion at the 1955 show.* (McC)

Left: *One of the major attractions in the centre ring is the military band.*

Below: *The Pegasus Band of the Parachute Regiment playing at the 1988 show.*

The Lancers and White Helmets get ready for action at the 1968 show. (DET)

Above: *Joe Tomlinson* (centre) *and Freddie Dix of the Chesterfield branch of the Parachute Regiment Association with Roy Marklew* (left) *who served in the 5th Royal Inniskillin Dragoon Guards, who helped with showground security.* (CU)

Left: *The Lifeguards performed at the 1970 show.*

Background image: *The Royal Marines Amphibious Arm of the Royal Navy performed at the 1975 show.*

ROYAL MARINES
AMPHIBIOUS ARM OF THE
ROYAL NAVY

dressed in grass skirts, armbands and anklets belying their strength. As the *Derbyshire Times* reported at the time:

They are as tough as they look, brave in battle and intensely loyal to the Crown. Also they are very keen on rugby and their drum major Sgt Epili Rayawa is an international. But they are all staunch methodists and they never play on a Sunday.

More fascinating still was the Frontier Pipe Band from Pakistan who came the following year direct from the Royal Tournament on their way to the Edinburgh Tattoo. Formed in 1913, the band was plucked from an armed civil force recruited from the tough tribesmen, the Khattaks and the Mahsubds, who lived in the legendary Khyber Pass. It was their job to patrol the rugged mountains and tortuous passages leading to Afghanistan and to try to keep peace in a country where the blood feud is still the order of the day. The tribal dances – the Khattaks with swords and the Mahsuds with rifles – were designed to whip up the emotions and rekindle the killer instinct on the eve of battle. But it wasn't the passion of the performers that caused the problem for show secretary Bill Conway – it was the rations list. The band's request for 112lbs of atta flour, 10lbs dahl, 14lbs ghee and exotic spices seriously overtaxed local suppliers. He told the local paper:

It's not really surprising that local shops cannot provide garam masala, dalchini sticks, dried tamarind, cavenda, korum and beetle nut – but happily now everything has been arranged.

That, however, wasn't the end of his troubles; when the arrangement was first made he was told the Pathans would have to cook over an open fire, which, as they were being billeted at a local school, could have proved a bit dangerous. That problem was solved when they were taught how to use gas rings. But there was another problem... Pathans are strict Muslims and their meat had to be killed in accordance with strict religious practice: 'Luckily we had a butcher in Sheffield who had a Muslim working on his staff who can kill sheep in the correct way.' It says a

A demonstration of military bravery.

lot for the progress of racial integration that today both the spices and the Halal meat would be readily available locally.

Whether the request was 'a bridge too far' for the secretary is not documented, but according to records the show stuck to home-grown bands for its military entertainment after that – with the exception of the Band of the US Air Forces in Europe – a descendent of the Glenn Miller Band, which appeared in 1980.

In 1977 plans for the Queen's Silver Jubilee posed unexpected problems for the show; every time secretary Ted Brownhill attempted to book a team from the Army, Navy or Air Force, he was met with a polite refusal. With the show just five months away he had been turned down by the Household Cavalry, the Royal Military Police, 12 military bands and even the RAF police dog display team, all of whom were standing by for royal duties. In the end he managed to attract the Royal Marines freefall parachute team and settled for music from the Southern Youth Highland Pipe and Drum Band.

Fl.-Lt John Lacey was one of the busiest men on the showground that day. He commanded the Royal Navy helicopter which staged a spectacular parachute jump and simulated rescue in the main arena then he was back down to earth grooming his wife Rosalind's horse Drake's Magic Star before she went on to win the National Westminster Stakes showjumping competition.

Five years later military activity in the South Atlantic put organisers in limbo again – as the countdown to the show began there was some doubt as to whether the units booked to appear would make it. The task force had included large contingents, not only of Royal Marines and Commandoes, but also of Welsh Guards. Then, with less than a week to go, the society was assured that the Welsh Guards Band, who didn't accompany the regiment on the *QEII*, and the Royal Artillery Motor Cycle Display Team would still be performing at Bakewell.

It was a sensitive time which led police to tighten security and although none of the soldiers who had seen active service were among the display team, one of the helicopters which saw action to regain the Falklands was there.

Over the next few years the Welsh Guards, the Royal Marines, the Bands of the Worcestershire and Sherwood Foresters, Queen's Lancashire Regiment, and the Cheshire Regiment all appeared at the show along with commando display teams, helicopter rescue, motorcycle displays and the K9 war dog team. On one occasion the assistant director Brian Bakel recalls standing at the door of the show office with the director John Smallman when the military contingent for that year went past:

We stood there and watched the Army, Navy and Airforce go by and commented that we hoped Britain didn't go to war that day, we'd never win because all the defences were at Bakewell Show. That was the year that half a submarine came and we had enormous difficulty getting it into the show-ground. Eventually we found a way through the Coombes Road entrance.

Sadly, as the Ministry of Defence trims down its operations, the appearance of military bands and other services-related entertainment such as the Royal Artillery Motorcycle Display Team has been trimmed down too. In years gone by it was an exciting way to recruit young people as well as a good PR exercise by the military. Today they simply can't afford it.

To bring one of the top bands of yesteryear to Bakewell Show in the twenty-first century would cost in excess of £10,000 by the time accommodation and travel has been paid for, which is why in recent years the show has been very pleased to welcome the talented and very popular Band of the Yorkshire Volunteers. Their scarlet uniforms make a brilliantly colourful contribution to the centre ring, but sadly nothing on the scale of the Household Cavalry or Fijian warriors.

The Army is still represented – in 2002 a team of young soldiers gave a demonstration of abseiling and invited visitors to have a go. And at the president's dinner on the eve of the 2002 show soldiers on the showground donned their ceremonial uniforms to present an impressive display of drumming with fluorescent drumsticks which lit up in the darkened marquee.

But there is one military connection which the show can never forget – the contribution of members of the Chesterfield branch of the Parachute Regiment Association. Following a few problems at the 1995 show they were asked if they would come and give support to security staff. Volunteers in their distinctive blazers and red berets proved a force to be reckoned with as they firmly but politely took control – a little too firmly for the poor president that first year. The Earl of Burlington and his mother the Marchioness of Hartington were stopped from coming in by Chesterfield branch president Major Bob Bragg because they didn't have tickets. They were escorted to the show office to get the necessary passes.

The Paras, many of them well into their seventies and a few in their eighties, worked on the showground for five years, their numbers swelled towards the end by the Royal Engineers and the Tank Regiment associations. But 2000 proved to be their last show. Bowing out their liaison officer Bill Gilliland admitted: 'I'm afraid we are just getting too old.'

A military display at the show.

❦ Twelve ❦

The Showground

Nestling in the beautiful Wye Valley, Bakewell Showground is one of the prettiest in the country and so many miles away from the field in Chesterfield where the first show was held back in 1819. Even the following year when it decamped to the yard and land surrounding the Rutland Arms at Bakewell, the actual showground bore no resemblance to what it is today. Since those early years the show has moved around the county until finally settling on a place to call home.

Initially the two original venues were adequate, but as the show grew they proved too small. When the Duke of Rutland built a new Cattle Market in Bakewell, it was decided to move from the Rutland Arms to where there was room to grow further. Lack of space caused problems in Chesterfield too – the town was expanding and organisers were forced to use several different crofts around the town. By the mid-1830s the society had attracted so many entries from around the county that there was a plea from the contingent in the south for the show to be staged in their area so they didn't have as far to travel. It was decided that perhaps the whole society was becoming too big and unwieldy and would benefit from having two organisations, one for the north and one for the south. So the south got its 'home' show and a new society too. According to records the show was held in the Chesterfield area for the last time in 1839.

The following year, in a break from tradition, it was staged at Alfreton Park, home of the 1839 president W. Palmer-Morewood. One of the most consistent supporters of the society, he had argued that because of lack of transport people in that part of the county had never seen an agricultural show and the 16 miles between Alfreton and Bakewell was just too far to walk there and back in one day.

The show continued to grow. Produce and pigeons and poultry were introduced in the 1850s – they were exhibited under cover in the Market Hall and later in the Town Hall. By 1870 it was in three sections – cattle, sheep and pigs were in the Cattle Market, poultry, small livestock and produce in the market hall and horses, hunters and root crops in the Meadows. That year there was a simple jumping competition too. It was not an arrangement which suited the punters who had to move from place to place and it brought a lot of complaints. Something had to be done, so a decision was taken to move the whole show to the

Meadows, a spacious 24-acre site on Belper Road. The same year, 1879, the annual dinner was held for the first time in a marquee on the showground with catering by Thomas Higgott of the Red Lion Hotel.

There followed a period of relative stability as far as the showground was concerned until after the First World War. The minutes of the meeting held on 9 February 1925 record the secretary reading a letter from Bakewell Urban District Council confirming that the Recreation Ground (formerly the Meadows) would be available for the annual show – but permission was unnecessary, for plans were already afoot to find the ever-growing show a new home.

A field called 'The Twenty Acres' next to Coombs Road in Bakewell was the perfect spot. Show organisers negotiated with the landlord and Bakewell butcher Charles Critchlow who tenanted the land and it was agreed to move the entire show the following year. In addition two supporters with fields adjacent to the plot – Mr Barker of The Brooklands and Duncan Orme – both offered the use of their land too. Little did organisers realise what an historic site they had inherited. A report into the showground, commissioned during the development of Bakewell Agricultural Business Centre, found land once known as Grammer Croft with evidence of preserved ridge-and-furrow formation. They also found continuation of an earthwork defining a tenth-century Saxon 'burh'. Further excavation unearthed a rare leather work shoe from around 1800. It was well worn, much repaired and had evidently been cut down later to be worn as a mule. It was found buried with fragments of chicken bone and larchwood carpenters' waste.

When the show moved to its new home, the administration – office work and meetings – continued to be carried out in a room at the Haddon Estates offices in Rutland Square, but as the estate workload grew, organisers were asked to find somewhere else. Fortunately an office was offered by the society's printers, J. Smith and Sons.

After the Second World War there is evidence that the showground was used other than at show times – in 1944 there are reports of a horse show, gymkhana and race meeting in aid of the Red Cross, Agriculture and RAF Benevolent Funds. In the wake of the war the show was very keen to support the Red Cross and also organised a special fund-raising sale at which

Bakewell Agricultural Business Centre across the centre ring – now an integral part of the showground.

Above: *An overview of the showground before the advent of the Agricultural Centre.*

cattle, sheep, pigs, goats, poultry, rabbits, dogs... and a kitten, came under the hammer. Other items donated by the townspeople of Bakewell included a grand-mother clock from Dr and Mrs Platts of Grindleford, a dinner gong from Mr C. Webster of Grange Mill and a toy rabbit from a Miss Pardoe of Bakewell. But probably the most unusual was an ink stand made from the hoof of a horse named Leap Year which died in 1869 – the kind donation of Mr Charles Boot of Thornbridge Hall.

At the 1947 show the Army came to the show's rescue by building two Bailey bridges over the River Wye and the mill-stream. The committee's thanks – 'to the commanding officers and all the ranks of the 106 and 129 Field Engineer Regiments (TA) who came over from Somme Barracks, Sheffield to erect the bridges on the footpath onto the showground' – are recorded in the minutes.

By 1952 the society had decided to erect a new river bridge to cope with ever-increasing numbers. The *Derbyshire Times* recorded at the time:

For some years one of the complaints visitors have made is the congestion that occurs on the footbridge leading to the ground that crossed the River Wye and the millstream. Although it is now a few years since these were widened and rebuilt they have not proved enough to cope with the crowds.

A car on the Bailey bridge.

In an effort to overcome this the society has, this year, had an additional bridge erected over the river and the millstream. It is hoped this will prove suffi-cient to eliminate the congestion of previous years.

Another out-of-show event was staged in 1952 – the prestigious Derbyshire County Rugby Football Union match against Staffordshire. Rugby was to become synonymous with Bakewell showground – as the home of the Old Mannerians.

More improvements followed in coronation year when, with membership at its highest giving the society money to invest, the permanent road from Coombs Road to the centre ring was extended, a mile of water pipes laid and electricity taken to many parts of the ground. Two years later there was another programme of ground improvements and repair work to be carried out following the deluge of 1954. Some 300 tons of stone and 120 tons of topsoil were laid, the ground was drained and re-seeded and two new entrances created, one for trade vehicles off Coombs Road and another for the public off Haddon Road.

A Bailey bridge was used again in 1956 when it was thrown across the River Wye near the pumping station to get traffic to the showground from the south side. The 1957 show suffered another torrential downpour and as soon as it was over anti-weather efforts began with a 2,000-yard network of drains installed at a cost of £1,000. That was not the only expenditure at that time. Still more land was needed for the show and car parking. So when Riverside Farm came onto the market in 1958 the society decided to buy it in order to get hold of a six-acre field adjacent to the showground. The actual farm and unwanted farm buildings were later sold off and nine further acres nearby were bought. By now the showground had a total of 42 acres of owned and leased land.

Increasing numbers of visitors brought increasing numbers of problems, particularly with traffic. In 1963 a 600-yard stretch of road was laid from one end of the showground to the other in a bid to clear up the jams and a further acre-and-a-half was reclaimed near the river bend to create more space. At the same time the Civil Defence had laid five miles of cables for the show's telephone and radio communication.

The organisation was growing so rapidly that it soon became obvious that the administration could no longer be carried out in various rented offices in the town. It was now big business and the show needed a properly-equipped base for the secretary and his staff. They got planning permission to build the cedarwood office, which is still the centre of the show's administration. It cost just £1,718 to build with electricity and main drainage extra. At the same time a further 1,220 yards of roadway was laid. As the *Derbyshire Times* observed at the time it 'indicated a firm trend towards independence'.

Another Bailey bridge was brought into service in 1967 – this time a double span for two-way traffic to try to ease the traffic congestion on the A6. Organisers had great difficulty getting hold of it, but with just days to spare it was in place and ready for use.

Maintenance and improvements continued throughout the late 1960s and '70s. Then in 1981 there was potential for disaster. The whole show had come under threat with proposals for a Bakewell bypass, which would effectively have sliced through the showground. Show director John Smallman gave evidence at a public enquiry and happily the plans were dropped. He said afterwards: 'I am happy and delighted that the bypass is a dead duck. We have the nicest setting in the United Kingdom and we aim to keep it that way.' 'Keeping it that way' was not easy and certainly not cheap. In 1985, in the wake of the Bradford Football Club tragedy, new fire precautions were introduced. Canvas seats around the main stand were replaced with wooden ones, gangways in the

1,578-seater main stand were widened and stewards given extra fire training – all at considerable cost to the society.

In 1987 new hardcore roads were installed with improved drainage, followed in 1988 by new underground cables. It is doubtful whether this expenditure had been built into calculations, but was a problem the society had to face sooner rather than later. One of the trade stands was erecting a flagpole which touched some live wires and plunged nearby houses into darkness. Health-and-safety representatives inspected the site and suggested that all the power cables should be insulated – or laid underground. Organisers decided to bite the bullet and carry out the underground work. It cost £11,500 – £1,000 more than the previous year's profit. It was the start of a two-year programme of significant capital expenditure on the showground. As well as the electrical work there was a new combined ring number two and new sumps for the toilets. In his annual report show director John Smallman commented:

The showground is rather like the Forth Bridge – there is always money to be spent trying to improve the facilities at the show for all who use them. This has been achieved without disturbing our sinking fund and that is no small achievement.

It was 'all hands to the pump' following the 1993 show – another one of appalling weather. That autumn a 'repair party' gathered on the showground on two

The inside of the Cattle Market – now the permanent home for the livestock entries.

The grandstand waiting for the visitors to arrive.

Sunday mornings and, with the help of a tractor, trailer and loader brought to the showground by president Richard Morten they carted soil from Big Bend to fill in the large holes and ruts created by cars stranded in the mud on show days. And on two Sundays in the spring they did it again.

Following the 1995 success of a new layout to create the agricultural quarter, further improvements were made in 1996. But there were behind-the-scenes discussions going on which were to have a huge impact on the show... the building of Bakewell Agricultural Business Centre on the showground. It was another three years before it became a reality. Bulldozers moved onto the site within weeks of the 1997 show ending and contractors Henry Boot battled on through what was one of the wettest autumns and winters in recent years to transform 12 acres at one end of the site into the new business centre. The project, which also involved a new access road off the A6 and a new bridge, was handed over with days to spare before the 1998 show.

In practical terms the showground had been turned around. The cattle, sheep and goats which were under canvas at the far end of the site were brought in to purpose-built pens in the new centre. The dogs, pigeons and poultry which had been displaced were given a much bigger and more easily accessible area at the Haddon Road end. There was now a much bigger agricultural area with 20 per cent more trade stands. The British food and farming marquee was much bigger and had been repositioned not far from the Coombs Road entrance. There were one or two teething problems, but the development effectively gave the society a superb launch pad for the show into the new millennium.

Over recent years the showground has been used for a number of out-of-show activities – some have succeeded, some have not. Regular car-boot sales proved popular and brought in much-needed income. One relatively recent event is a twice-yearly garden festival in the spring and autumn, which draws an increasing number of visitors. Drainage and maintenance work has continued and without weather problems the site would now be in prime condition. But disastrous flooding in 2002 made the showground the wettest anyone can remember, causing untold problems – and expense. Organisers will battle on, weary with the weather, but still safe in the knowledge that, rain or no rain, Bakewell Show still has the prettiest showground in the UK.

Above left and right and below: *Eric Chandler takes care of the electrics on the showground* (CU); *erecting the staging in the late 1960s.*

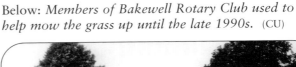

Below: *Members of Bakewell Rotary Club used to help mow the grass up until the late 1990s.* (CU)

Right: *Erecting a large marquee in the late 1960s.*

❧ Thirteen ❧
Food and Farming

It was originally intended as a one-off to celebrate British Food and Farming Year in 1989, but Bakewell's food and farming marquee has long since established itself as one of the most high-profile exhibits on the showground. Despite being at the mercy of the weather – sweltering in the heat and sinking into the mud in the rain because of a spring underneath the site – food and farming is still a magnet for visitors to the show who enjoy specialist British food.

The first food and farming committee was chaired by show stalwart Willis White and included Sandy Boyd who managed Chatsworth Farm Shop and a flamboyant character called Peter Pugson who ran his delicatessen and wine business in Buxton, as well as local specialist cheese makers and others who were interested in British food. Mary Morten, wife of joint director Richard Morten, was co-opted at the second meeting and went on to chair the committee for several years. Peter Pugson was an inspired choice for this committee. A founder member of the UK Cheese Guild, he was a passionate promoter of specialist cheeses and was delighted to see the re-emergence of the specialist cheese maker. He would go to any lengths to try new samples and support the small cheese maker – even to the point of knocking on the doors of complete strangers.

That first year a small tent was erected for the new food and farming exhibit with the cheese competition held in a tunnel at one end, and Chatsworth Farm Shop with its suppliers filling the trade stands. How things have changed. Today the marquee is four times as large and has been split into four distinct sections. The trade stand area now attracts around 40 specialist food producers from all over the country selling a variety of things from venison and pork to fudge, coffee and lemonade. The emphasis is still very much on 'British', with exhibitors including Peak District Products and Belvoir Castle cordials, although there have been occasions when 'foreigners' have tried to slip in.

The debate about whether or not to let a man selling olives into the marquee raged for some time in the committee meetings before it was decided that he did not qualify. Interestingly in latter years it has reared its head again with a renewed 'local v global' argument.

The competition tent now includes meat products such as sausages, pies and black pudding as well as cheese and it is an impressive display. There is keen competition both among the specialist cheese producers – who send their exhibits from all over the UK – and, since the introduction of the new section, among local sausage-producing butchers too.

It is a separate air-conditioned tent which makes it a popular venue for overheated visitors on show days. One regular visitor is the Duchess of Devonshire who for several years judged a special cheese competition called the Duchess' Choice. Her sister-in-law Lady Elizabeth Cavendish has also judged, along with personnel from other shows and representatives of the NFU.

Looking back over the show's history it would appear that cheese classes have always played a significant part in the event, which is not surprising since traditionally farmers and their wives have made cheese, not only because it was a good way to preserve nourishing summer milk, but also because it was a handy method of transporting country fayre to the city. Some, like a Mr W. Tagg of Dirtlow Farm, were very good at it. He is credited with having won the best farmhouse cheese for four years running – a feat which was recognised with a special silver trophy worth the equivalent of four first prizes. But the coming of the railways brought cheese production to Derbyshire on a large scale. The first cheese factory was founded just outside Derby in 1870 and at one time, of the seven UK cheese-making factories, six were in the county. Now there is only one: J.M. Nuttall of Hartington – part of Dairy Crest – where today they handmake stilton cheeses to sell all around the world. That factory was opened by the Duke of Devonshire in the mid-1800s and originally produced Derbyshire cheese. But when the Nuttall family – who had been making stilton in Melton Mowbray for a number of years – took over at the turn of the century production switched to stilton.

Why did so many of the other cheese factories close? The show's history gives a clue when it reports on a speech made at the 1879 annual dinner by the Duke of Rutland, in which he expressed his concern that strong competition from imported American cheese had meant the closure of several Derbyshire cheese factories, many of which had only been

Above: *The Lurgashall Winery – one of the exhibitors in the food and farming marquee.* (CU)

Below: *Chatsworth Farm Shop was the mainstay of the food and farming marquee in its early years.* (CU)

Above: *A selection of prizewinning cheeses in the cheese competition.* (CU)

Below: *Cumbrian home-cured farmhouse bacon exhibited in the food and farming marquee.* (CU)

operating for three or four years. The ones which did survive, however, appeared to be successful – at the close of the century it is interesting to note that the first and second prizewinners in the open cheese classes came, not from the ranks of farmers' wives and daughters, but from the Gratton Dairy Association and the Ivonbrook Grange Dairy Association. This result reflected another trend. Improved transport had led to an increased demand for milk and farmers' wives simply stopped making cheese. One seemingly lone survivor was Cheshire. The families in that county worked hard to keep the popular white and red varieties alive, and for a good number of years after the war the cheese classes were filled almost entirely with entries from Cheshire farms. But the die had been cast and few farmhouses made their own special cheese.

And if the knock-on effect of the Second World War had had anything to do with it, specialist cheese production would have been lost forever. The Ministry of Food laid down rules which placed the emphasis on cheapness and nourishment rather than taste. It had a devastating effect on the industry, particularly in Derbyshire, and by 1950 only 700 tons of cheese were produced – a quarter of pre-war production – and specialist cheese production had all but died out. Then in the 1960s it began to re-emerge as people rediscovered the joys of good old-fashioned tasty farmhouse cheeses.

Derbyshire cheese maker Bobby Clarke won first prize for her Peakland cheeses at the 1989 show. Bobby was on the food and farming committee for a number of years. (DET)

Recognising the re-birth of specialist cheese making, and latterly the skill of the meat products producer, has been a triumph for the food and farming committee – underlined by the number and quality of the entries each year and the popularity of the exhibit, which attracts a large percentage of the show's visitors. In 2002 the committee acknowledged the emergence of organic produce by adding classes for organic hard and soft cheeses and hoped to encourage an increased entry from goat- and sheep-cheese makers by having a new class for any variety of cheese made from unpasteurised milk.

Another popular area in the food and farming marquee, the demonstration theatre was originally established to show off skills such as meat cutting, cheese making and cake icing, but since then it has played host to a number of high-profile personalities, many of them thanks to the contacts of committee member Peter Pugson. Arguably the most important was the Tory Food Minister David MacLean who took part in a pre-show question-and-answer forum when he faced a number of extremely frustrated local farmers.

That evening was the forerunner of an eve-of-show event which continued to be staged until 2002. Following the Minister was chef Glyn Christian, descendent of Fletcher Christian of the notorious Mutiny of the Bounty, who came for two successive years – on the first occasion to give a talk and on the second to give a cookery demonstration on show day as well. His audience still remembers the anecdote about how he was left in agony after dashing off to the loo during ad breaks on a TV show, forgetting to wash his hands first... he'd been chopping chillies!

Bandana-wearing James Martin, the celebrity chef of Winchester's Hotel du Vin and a regular on TV's 'Ready, Steady, Cook', was popular too, despite his anecdotes being a bit too fruity for some of the audience. He dealt with one heckler by inviting him on to the stage to toast some breadcrumbs in a dry pan because the show kitchen equipment didn't include a grill. After the man had laboriously carried out the task he was dismissed by James who said he didn't really need them because he was going to make a lemon cheesecake. His problems were small compared with the one faced by TV chef Tessa Bramley. As the motherly demonstrator worked preparing food in front of the Tuesday-night audience, it started to rain heavily, which would not have been a problem had there not been a hole in the marquee directly above her prep table. As the rain dripped down Tessa simply moved operations across to a dry section and, like the consummate professional she is, she just carried on. She had once been demonstrating on the *QEII* when all the electrics went and there was a shortage of water, so, she told the audience, a drop of rain on her prep table was nothing.

But not all the star performers were as calm and accommodating – one arrived empty-handed and demanded that organisers supply her with a range of knives and utensils as well as a long shopping list of ingredients, sending them scurrying around their contacts to get things sorted out before the demonstration. She then outraged members of the WI who were in the audience by constantly running her fingers through her hair and then carrying on handling food, and later dunking her hot tired feet in the bain marie. Needless to say she was not invited back.

Above: *Keeping it in the family – Belvoir Cordials, produced by the late Duke of Rutland's brother Lord John Manners, regularly exhibited in the food and farming marquee. Lord John* (centre) *is pictured with the Duchess of Rutland* (right) *during her presidential year in 1991.* (CU)

Left: *Prizewinning cheese from J.M. Nuttall.* (CU)

Finding chefs for the two show days also proved problematic. At the 2000 show Richard Smith of Smiths of Sheffield was booked to appear, but found his application for a licence to extend his restaurant was due to be heard when he would have been on stage, so he pulled out. Another local chef on the programme suddenly left the hotel where he was working and organisers were forced to find two last-minute substitutes.

The Superchef competition was launched by the food and farming committee to try to find the area's best amateur chef. The first couple of years were a triumph, but after that local culinary experts seemed thin on the ground and the competition was abandoned through lack of entries.

Local Brownies have performed in the show kitchen – making pizza for their cook's badges – and one year the cast of the radio soap 'The Archers' re-created Ambridge for an after-show evening for fans. The kitchen for the theatre was provided by local suppliers who usually managed to sell it afterwards and the cooker by a company which brought cookers to the show anyway. But on one occasion the kitchen supplier went bankrupt less than a month before the show leaving a frantic committee to find a replacement – which happily they did.

Part of the food and farming committee's remit is to educate young people by promoting the link between farming and the countryside and each year a special corner is put aside for this purpose. Organisers try to make the journey from the plough to the plate as entertaining as possible and one year even managed to get a working model cow to demonstrate milking.

All food and farming activities need sponsorship, and unfortunately Bakewell Show isn't of a size which attracts the major supermarkets, which prefer to concentrate on events like The Royal or the Great Yorkshire. Committee members have become very good at getting 'in kind' sponsorship and limited amounts of 'cash' support. They organised a fashion show and for a couple of years held 'Ladies Who Lunch' events to try to raise money to support their exhibit. It is increasingly difficult, but the committee remained dedicated to its aim since it was set up – to celebrate British food and farming.

❧ Fourteen ❧

Other Attractions

With so much publicity given to the high-profile aspects of Bakewell Show – the livestock, dogs and horses – there is a danger that some of the gentler pursuits, such as Fisherman's Walk, could be overlooked. But tucked away in the south-east corner of the showground, this section is very much alive and... fishing! Established in 1968, it was run for a number of years by John Dudding, an angling enthusiast from Nottingham who first held a rod at the age of 11. By arrangement with the Duke of Rutland he had hoops and markers placed in the River Wye so that light-hearted distance and accuracy competitions could be held.

During the 1970s the highlights of the day were appearances by world fly-casting champion Jack Martin of Scarborough, who not only gave demonstrations of casting but also a commentary on technique. Further up the river there was a chance for everyone to try their hand at casting with free tuition and rods provided – an opportunity for those who have never had their hands on a rod before to have a go.

Mr Dudding, a retired chartered architect who was helped by his wife and Stanley Woodrow, spent many years fishing the River Wye and was a member of Chatsworth Fishery. He was still running the section when he was in his eighties.

Today Fisherman's Walk is run by Graham Walmsley. It is still a magnet for visitors, whether they are anglers or not. They get a practical insight into fishing as well as the opportunity to become a champion fly-caster. There are prizes for both adults and juniors and the excitement really builds up as the Thursday-afternoon deadline approaches and competitors try one more time to improve their performances. But it is not just the competitive element which appeals to visitors, there's also tuition by top anglers as well as demonstrations of intricate fly-tying by experts. It's no wonder that Fisherman's Walk is always an unmissable stop in the presidential tour.

Ostriches have become a regular feature of the show, but for exhibition only. Visitors can see the birds in their pen – and taste the meat at the ostrich burger stall next door! (CU)

If Fisherman's Walk is tucked away on the showground, the vintage vehicle and machinery display is certainly not! Vintage cars have pride of place on the Wednesday and motorcycles on Thursday. The vintage section is a paradise for farming historians and mechanical buffs alike with everything from beautifully restored cars to old tractors, equipment and engines. But even these machines are not as old as the ones on display at the early shows. Things such as John Spencer's improved hay and straw chopping machine, which he unveiled at the 1832 show, or the one-horse tipping cart with the $4^1/_2$in iron tyres which made an appearance two years later. And unlike the mid-1800s, when the show had to shift to Chatsworth to accommodate all the new machines on show, today's vintage section has a relatively modest pitch.

Vintage cars have been an attraction at the show for a number of years and visitors delight in seeing examples such as a 1929 Rolls Tourer complete with Angela Caravan, a Model T Ford of 1920 and a Humber Tourer.

Numbers in the motor bike section had been dwindling until the 2001 show when they enjoyed something of a revival. Vintage bike enthusiast Phil Crosby was so successful in filling one of the gaps left by the non-appearance of the livestock that he was invited to return to the 2002 show. Phil, who with Peter Mather has a collection of 50 bikes which he keeps in a former bakery in Matlock, managed to bring in around 60 machines from a 50-mile radius. But the star of the show was undoubtedly his own very rare 1906 Minerva, first registered in Sheffield and still with its original number-plate.

Above: *Taking a nap by the steam-engine display.*

Above right: *A gleaming vintage tractor.*

Right: *An owl demonstration at the 1988 show.* (DET)

Below: *A basket-weaving demonstration at the 2002 show.* (CU)

Background image: *Dry-stone-walling demonstration at the 1988 show.* (DET)

Robin Rhodes, president in 2002, gets a fly-fishing lesson at Fisherman's Walk. (CU)

❧ Fifteen ❧

Weather Watch

The Little Royal – long may it rain! A harsh headline, some may say, but not altogether undeserved. Regular downpours are as much a part of the rich tradition of Bakewell Show as flat caps, green wellies and waxed jackets. If the country had been struck by a drought for 364 days, show-goers could lay odds that they would be renewing the relationship with their long-lost brollies come show day.

It has been the same old story since records began. Way back in 1863, when the show was held on 10 October, the *Derbyshire Courier* reported that visitors were 'wading in a sea of mud with cattle and sheep standing in absolute misery.' The rain had fallen without let-up since the eve of the show, the only variation in conditions being that 'some of the rain fell perpendicularly and some of it fell slantingly with the wind.' Miserable conditions indeed for an agricultural show and the newspaper took organisers to task for failing to provide any shelter.

It was a message which evidently struck home, for the following year the show was staged with a marquee on the Meadows at Belper Road – although on this occasion the weather lurched to the opposite extreme and a number of livestock were overcome by the heat. In 1865 the show was back at the Cattle Market, but the society took the precaution of erecting boarding to ensure some shelter for both animals and humans in the case of either sun or rain (and to prevent would-be gatecrashers from getting a free view over the wall).

Another attempt to ensure more favourable conditions was made in 1885 when the show was held a month earlier than usual, on the first Thursday of September. It was a logical enough tactic, but the British weather is not that easily beaten: there were heavy showers throughout the day, 'considerably interfering with the comfort of the visitors.'

Measures to counteract extremes of temperature have always posed a problem for organisers. They expected the worst back in 1895 after one of the harshest winters on record. England's lowest ever temperature was reportedly measured at Buxton in February, but come summer it was a totally different story. Brilliant sunshine heralded one of the most successful shows of its day.

As we have recorded, the weather is the single most culpable factor when apportioning blame for the show's historically unstable financial status. There is nothing more guaranteed to keep visitors away in their droves than a wet show-day morning.

In 1906 near-tropical weather beamed on Bakewell, which welcomed some of the country's top livestock champions, fresh from success at the Royal Show which had been held in Derby that summer. But the following year spirits were dampened once again as incessant rain resulted in the lowest attendance for years, a deficit of £200 and the collapse of show secretary William Clark, attributed to 'overstrain and anxiety'. No doubt he was learning to cope with the stress by 1912 when the headlines again trumpeted the news: 'Bakewell Show drowned out.'

The elements have proved a fearsome enemy over the years, and sometimes the weather on show day itself has been almost irrelevant. The second postwar show, in 1947, was a case in point. This was renowned as the year of the Great Blizzard, which occurred in the first three months and devastated the farming industry across Britain. Severe crop damage meant that fodder and feeding stuffs were in acutely short supply and as roads were blocked by snow and ice, and villages cut off amidst the big freeze, deliveries of fodder, milk and other general supplies ground to a halt. There were enormous losses of livestock, with sheep farmers bearing the heaviest burden, and the animals which did survive were hardly prize beasts. In the wake of the crisis an Agricultural Disaster Fund was set up to help families struggling against the odds and the Bakewell Society made a generous donation of £100 to the fund's Derbyshire branch. But it took months for farmers to recover and the knock-on effects took their toll on that year's show.

Bakewell's show-goers are without doubt a loyal bunch. Many families turn out year after year without fail and a thorough drenching is considered merely part of the experience. But there is no doubt that the barometer is usually a pretty accurate measure of attendance figures – when the pressure drops, so do visitor numbers. In 1972, for example, a very bad day kept gate numbers down to just 11,918, a disastrous result for the show, and resulted in a £6,000 deficit and another appeal to members for donations.

Of course the converse is equally true when it comes to the weather, despite the fact that a hot, dusty showground, with only a sheet of sun-baked canvas to

Left: *One hot and sunny day – one day pouring with rain... the torrent at the 1984 show.* (SN)

Below: *The day before the 2002 show.* (CU)

Below left: *The day after the 2002 show.* (CU)

Centre left: *Show-goers always come prepared with macs and brollies – a scene from the 1986 show.* (SN)

Bottom left: *Keeping cool the cowboy way.* (SN)

Bottom right: *Keeping cool the doggy way.* (SN)

Background image: *The sun shines on the 1984 show.* (SN)

protect one from the sizzling heat, can be a pretty uncomfortable experience on a sweltering August day. Such was the case in 1955, which dawned bright and sunny, drawing the highest one-day show attendance in the society's history. A paying gate of a whopping 46,779 was recorded, putting it firmly among the so-called 'golden years' of the 1950s, when three shows clocked up attendances in excess of 40,000 and most others were not far behind.

In 1952 the sun shone on Bakewell Show and by 10a.m. 30,000 people had pushed their way through the turnstiles. At that point the heavens opened and confusion took over as everyone ran for cover. Some of the happiest visitors that year were the mackintosh and rubber-boot sellers who did a roaring trade. Exactly 20 years later it was the same old story and the busiest spot on the showground was the umbrella stand where 200 brollies had been sold before lunch.

In spite of the show's popularity at the time, 1954 was one of the wettest years. Overnight rain had turned the main pathways into muddy lanes and over 200 tons of hardcore and gravel had to be spread over them before visitors could be admitted. Even so, vehicles arriving on the showground soon found themselves stuck fast in the mire. Several SOS messages had to be broadcast over the loudspeakers, appealing for staff to go to the rescue, and dozens of cars and vans were towed out by a team of tractors lined up by show surveyor Mr D.A. Fisher who, with remarkable foresight, had come up with the master plan. 'We began to get alarmed last Thursday about the state of the ground,' he told the *Derbyshire Times*. 'We started to put heaps of gravel at strategic points and two tractors stood by in case they were needed.' Eleventh-hour orders for hardcore and grit were placed with five quarry companies and late on Wednesday night last-minute preparations were still going on. Mr Fisher joined forces with Inspector S. Brearley of Bakewell Police to prevent even more chaotic conditions. Between them they switched the cattle wagon entrance in a bid to avoid an acute left-hand bend which had already been churned up by early arrivals.

Things had improved very little two years later when the event was labelled 'one of the greatest battles against the weather in the long history of the Little Royal.' For ten days contractors and workmen were engaged in a struggle against gale-force winds which ripped down tents, and torrential rain and

A brolly shared... watching the horse display at the 1985 show. (SN)

thunderstorms which left a trail of soaked canvas and pools of surface water. The River Wye had swollen to such an extent that low-lying fields were completely flooded. Again it fell to the hapless Mr Fisher to lead the fight against the elements. In an operation of military precision, he ordered the spreading of 200 tons of stone and gravel and 60 tons of sand to surface the main routes. Wire meshing and steel tracks were thrown down at the approaches to the car park and the south side of the show-ground, to prevent vehicles sinking axle-deep in the quagmire. As rain finally began to subside in the run-up to the show, the drains were tapped to take away surface water. 'In view of the abominable weather, it is really remarkable that the showground was ready on time,' admitted Mr Fisher. And although a two-foot-deep furrow was churned up in the broad, ringside avenue, it still didn't put off the thousands who turned up as usual for their annual outing.

That certainly wasn't the case by the following year, although perhaps, by that time, long-suffering show-goers had simply had enough of the rain. In 1957 a torrential cloudburst hit the show at 12.45p.m. and sent thousands scurrying for cover. From then on it poured non-stop and people were left huddling beneath trees and even seeking shelter beneath the floor of the grandstand, while others simply gave up and went home.

For those who stayed it was a curtailed centre-ring programme with only the showjumping surviving the downpour – the Grand Parade and a display by the RASC and the King's African Rifles were both cancelled after troops were drenched in an earlier parade. At teatime the big mud-bath began as cars and lorries struggled to leave the showground and as early as 4p.m. messages were going out to Mr Fisher: 'This is going to cost the society hundreds of pounds in tractors and labour hire.'

Sadly the event's success in its 'fifties heyday' was not reflected in its profits. In record-breaking 1955 the excess of income over expenditure was a mere £140, which triggered a major organisational re-think and a desperate search for ideas which might boost takings while also cutting back on outgoings.

In the 1970s the local press coined the phrase 'Bakewell's rain jinx' after a spate of wet show days. Following the record washout of 1972, organisers held their breath when, just two years later, violent storms at 5a.m. heralded yet another disaster, threatening to turn the showground into a muddy morass. But dry weather in the run-up to the event meant the fields were dry and the deluge didn't cause as many problems as had been feared.

There followed a couple of hot years when ice-cream sellers and sun hats took over as the most profitable goods on sale. But 1977 brought the start of yet another wet run, lasting into the 1980s, and signalling the need for drastic action.

The formal move to a two-day show was calculated to improve visitor numbers but also served as effective damage limitation on the weather front, halving the risk of a washout in one fell swoop. If there was torrential rain on Wednesday, then what the heck! There was a 50:50 chance of it being dry on Thursday – which was exactly what happened in 1982 but in reverse, leading to a stream of complaints on one day about excessive dust, followed by a flood of grumbles the next about excessive mud. It was a real no-win situation. Unfortunately the weather gambit failed to pay off for the first full two-day event in 1980, which was swamped by heavy rain and appalling ground conditions on both days. Numbers paying on the gate were down by more than 10,000 that year and profits tumbled accordingly, into a deficit of £5,455. However, true disaster was averted by a rise in the number of patrons and members and a growth in sponsorship too.

The rain didn't trouble seasoned show-goers, of course, who were well accustomed to the wet and dressed accordingly. The *Sheffield Morning Telegraph* reported:

The Duchess of Devonshire arrived in mackintosh, wellies and a fetching yachting cap. Her footwear was marginally upstaged by Lady Caroline Waterhouse who lived up to her name with a dashing pair of yellow wellingtons.

And while the steady downpour may not have bothered visitors, it did put a dampener on the president's lunch. The salt got so dank that VIP guests had to prise off the silver tops of the salt cellars and fork out the contents – marginally less embarrassing for the caterers than in 1984 when this same event came to grief after thunder turned the cream sour.

Things finally looked up in 1981 and the so-called jinx was broken with a gloriously sunny show. The good weather was a welcome relief after so many damp squibs, but the sun too has been responsible for its fair share of problems over the years.

In 1989 high temperatures caused a headache for organisers when the centre ring cracked in the heat and tons of topsoil and sand had to be put down to protect the valuable horses taking part in showjumping events. The following year local media reported that more than 100 people had needed treatment for the effects of heat, and livestock had to be hosed down to keep them cool – apart from the unfortunate sheep and dogs which had already been groomed, fluffed and beribboned ready for their respective competitions. The heatwave continued in 1991 when some cattle and sheep had to be sent home early, suffering from sunburn. The warm weather takes its toll on humans too, as demonstrated in 1995 by a *Sheffield Star* report: 'Tempers boiled over at the start of the normally sedate Bakewell Show,' it read, continuing:

Soaring temperatures contributed to an outbreak of road rage in the car park. One woman fell out with another motorist over a parking space and threatened to spray paint a show dog...

Police had to be called in to resolve the dispute.

One of the worst years in recent times was 1993 when a series of setbacks conspired to make life difficult for organisers. For a start heavy rain fell for days as preparations got underway and organisers had to work until midnight to avoid disaster after the floral-art tent sprang a leak. Then a 70-ton trailer-load of straw, intended to help mop up the puddles, went up in flames the night before the show. A lorry bringing replacements was stuck in a tailback of traffic, queueing to get into the rain-sodden ground the following morning. And to cap the lot, an icy wind blew up, pulling a hot-air balloon from its mooring and flattening smaller tents across the site. Normally unflappable secretary Ted Brownhill commented: 'In 18 years I don't remember us having to surmount the difficulties we've had this year. I certainly don't remember vehicles having to be towed in!'

In 1997 when storms and floods swamped the West Country, Honiton Show was among a number of events which were cancelled as a result and cider maker Steve Gilman found himself all revved up with nowhere to go. So he jumped into his lorry, drove overnight and managed to secure a pitch at Bakewell Show... where the sun shone all day.

These days the effects of the weather have, thankfully, been minimised by the construction of permanent buildings on site. The new Agricultural Business Centre provides covered accommodation for livestock and indoor space for some stands and exhibitions. The new roads and car parks which formed part of the project offer far easier access for motor vehicles as well as a welcome alternative to muddy fields on wet days. But the character of the show, with its acres of tents and picturesque setting, still remains unchanged.

Sixteen

The Show Must Go On

Palls of black smoke, rising from the pyres of cattle and sheep slaughtered in the aftermath of the most recent foot-and-mouth outbreak, will long haunt Britain's farming communities. The devastating consequences of the 2001 epidemic were played out in full public view, with extensive television and newspaper coverage of day-to-day developments and the people whose lives were scarred by the crisis. Feelings ran high, both within the industry and beyond, as the far-reaching effects of the disease were mulled over and debated in the lofty parliamentary halls of Europe and Westminster and in local pubs, shops and workplaces nationwide.

The long-term repercussions of the outbreak are still rumbling on. No corner of the land was left untouched as draconian restrictions were imposed in a bid to halt the spread of the disease. Farms were cordoned off, communities isolated, footpaths closed and businesses decimated as visitors turned their backs on the countryside. As the crisis grew, show organisers all over Britain faced a dilemma: on the one hand were the months of preparation and expectation which had already gone into their events, on the other, the seemingly insurmountable obstacles and huge financial losses involved if they went ahead. One by one they weighed up the odds, then most admitted defeat and cancelled their shows. But not Bakewell.

The committee agonised long and hard over what to do for the good of the show – and for the good of the community. There were no cases of foot and mouth in Derbyshire, but that could change at any moment and restrictions on the movement of livestock, coupled with the farmers' natural fears for their animals, made the prospect of a traditional agricultural show almost laughable.

It was a tough choice but a decision had to be made, and once made there was no going back. In the end it was the plight of the rural community as a whole which made up the committee's mind: the show must go on, but without the livestock. 'Although we respected other shows deciding to cancel because of the crisis, we felt we had to carry on,' said joint director Brian Bakel, continuing:

Farmers needed a day out, away from the pressures they faced, and we saw a way of helping local traders, who had suffered so badly from the knock-on effects of foot and mouth. We knew that year's Bakewell Show would be different, but it would help to bring the community together at a difficult time for everyone.

In the end the event was rebranded as 'Bakewell Show – Backing the British Countryside'. In deference to the farmers there were no cloven-hoofed livestock on site, but pigeon, poultry and rabbit classes went ahead as usual and the dog show attracted a record entry. Horticulture, the food and farming exhibition and other non-livestock-related attractions were unaffected and a packed programme of entertainment made sure there was plenty to bring in the crowds.

Bakewell's loyal supporters turned out in their thousands as usual, along with many newcomers. Each farmer who normally brought his stock to the show received a free family ticket. A special area was set aside as an 'Open for Business' exhibition where local companies, suffering as a result of the slump in Peak District tourism, could display their products and services free of charge. This element proved so successful that it has now been taken up by the Federation of Small Businesses and is a regular feature of the show.

This most recent outbreak of foot and mouth is still fresh in the minds of those living in and around the countryside, but it is by no means an isolated incident. Over the course of its history Bakewell Show has had to cope with disease on a regular basis, and not always with such a satisfactory outcome.

The first disease to cause problems was rinderpest, or cattle plague, which swept the country in 1866. No horned stock could be exhibited because of the risk of infection and the quality of cattle at the show was affected for some years to come. Rinderpest was a new but relatively short-lived threat to the nation's livestock – the virus had been virtually eradicated within a decade and the last recorded case in the UK was in 1877 – but at the time it was a major concern. Usually fatal, it accounted for the loss of whole herds of cattle, bringing ruin to many farms. There was no compensation system in operation at first and many dairy herds were wiped out, leaving their farmers in desperate financial difficulties. Later, the Derbyshire Cattle Plague Association was set up to secure them some support, but it was small comfort to those who had already sacrificed their livelihoods.

Foot and mouth first appeared in Britain in the 1830s but did not make its impact felt at Bakewell until 1875. It was widespread in Derbyshire at that time and many farmers thought the show should have been cancelled as a result. Despite loudly-voiced fears of the risks involved it went ahead, in a way which would have been unthinkable today. Entry to competitive classes was restricted to animals from farms which were known to be free of disease and only a small number of cloven-hoofed animals were put forward. Farmers were no doubt rightly concerned about the risks of bringing their livestock into contact with people from infected areas.

There was no let-up in the disease and by 1881 foot and mouth had taken hold across the length and breadth of the country. The result was a fall in the number of entries, which was further compounded the following year. By 1883 things were so serious that the show was cancelled altogether – the only time in its history that this has happened.

Farmers were desperate to protect their herds or to cure those already infected and there was a rash of curious recipes and remedies all claiming to bring about the desired effect. Among the most common measures were dosing with hay tea, gruel or linseed tea. There was also a procedure which involved leading infected stock through a trough of quicklime and dressing their sores with Stockholm tar. Some so-called experts recommended swabbing the animals' mouths several times a day with a watery solution of tincture of myrrh, while others dismissed these practices as quack medicine and preferred simply to leave their sick livestock to rest on a dry floor with plenty of clean litter.

Whatever the solution, things finally began to improve and the show was back in 1884 when entries were down but quality was up, according to records. A decade later the compulsory slaughter of cattle infected by foot and mouth was made law, but that year it was swine fever which hit the county and pig classes had to be dropped from the schedule. Swine fever was another recurrent problem for show organisers. It proved troublesome again in 1902 and this time the Board of Agriculture ruled that pig classes must be cancelled at all shows that summer. In fact, bouts of the disease caused disruption with such regularity over the years that moves were eventually made to drop pigs from the schedule altogether. The final straw came in 1974 when an outbreak of swine vesicular disease put paid to any lingering hopes of sustaining the section.

Organisers lived up to their reputation for resilience in 1952 when they were faced with not one but three problems. The pigeon and poultry competitions were cancelled early on after an outbreak of fowl pest – a precursor to years of trouble from this particular disease. 'Several poultry shows in the 1950s had to be cancelled because of outbreaks of fowl pest,'

recalls Frank Clarke, chairman of the small livestock committee for over 20 years. 'A consequence of this disease's persistence was that from 1966 until 1972 all birds sent for exhibition had to be vaccinated against it.' It was a precaution which evidently paid dividends, for there has been no such problem in recent years. However, in 1952 it was only the beginning of the troubles. Foot and mouth was again reported in the area – and no sooner had the all-clear been given than an outbreak of swine fever took a grip. Rumours began to circulate that the show would have to be cancelled, but officials were determined to go ahead. In traditional Bakewell style they got their way, although it was decided to cancel all classes for animals considered to be at risk: cattle, sheep, goats and pigs. Livestock was consequently restricted to just horses and dogs, but the show's customary Dunkirk spirit prevailed and the faith of organisers proved justified when entries for the remaining classes reached 2,786.

A ten-hour programme of centre-ring events was laid on to draw the crowds, but attendance was predictably depleted by the somewhat limited range of attractions. Thankfully things were almost back to normal the following year, with only the poultry missing and a record number of entries overall.

For the next decade swine fever was the only real problem, but foot and mouth struck once again in 1966. This time some classes went ahead unscathed while it all but obliterated others. There was a silver lining for Tom Nadin of Ashbourne: he was the only farmer able to bring his gritstone sheep and swept the board, walking off with the ram, lamb and shearing prizes. By the following year the outbreak had reached epidemic proportions and October 1967 went down as the most concentrated incidence of the disease recorded in the UK to date. Derbyshire was one of the worst affected counties and general life was severely disrupted, with even the society's annual dinner being called off. Fortunately the worst was over by spring 1968, but the disease had left an indelible mark, with the Government refusing to vaccinate and more than 400,000 livestock slaughtered in a bid to halt its spread.

That year it was the Ministry of Agriculture which disrupted the show, with its brucellosis eradication scheme. Strict regulations brought in to control this disease, affecting cattle and goats, included a 60-day isolation clause which hit farmers hard and resulted in a 30 per cent drop in show entries. However, Bakewell was not so severely hit as other shows, which reported decreases in entries of up to 40 per cent.

And so the cycle goes on. As foot and mouth declined there was widespread self-congratulation that it was finally on the retreat. But recent events have shown the disease is far from beaten – and the increasingly global nature of the farming industry suggests there could well be new problems to overcome. No doubt Bakewell, like other shows all over the country, will have many more challenges to face in the future.

Seventeen

The Main Attraction

No show is complete without its star turn and Bakewell is no exception, although centre-ring attractions have varied immensely over the years. In the early days there was no need to put on a special crowd-puller – Victorian farmers were more than happy to turn out merely for the chance to show off their prize pigs and cattle. But by the turn of the century things were starting to change. The first special events took the form of simple jumping competitions. These events were soon expanded to include trotting and galloping races which were hugely popular with both farmers and spectators. Crowds would turn out to see the horses as they raced flat-out for the finishing line at the end of a one-and-a-half-mile

Sheen Farmers, world champions at tug-o'-war in 1975, 1976 and 1977.

(RON DUGGINS)

course and excitement reached fever pitch as bets changed hands on the likely outcome. In 1901 13 horses lined up for the Open Trotting Handicap which took off from the Meadows after the main business of the day, at 4p.m. The rules stated that a bell would ring five minutes before the start of each heat and a pistol shot would signal the start of the race. Any competitor not on the starting line at that point would forfeit his place and anyone who jumped the gun would be disqualified.

The final was hotly contested by the two heat winners and the two fastest losers, all in the running for a prize: there was £21 for the first home, £7.10s. for the runner-up, £3.3s. for third place and £1 for fourth. The event was followed by the Open Galloping Race, held over a mile-long course, which attracted another 13 hopefuls and equal fervour among the betting public. Trotting races continued to be a regular feature until the Second World War, when they were abandoned in favour of more commercial attractions. They enjoyed a fleeting revival in 1967 when the races were reintroduced instead of senior showjumping. But the switch triggered a flood of complaints and finally sounded the death-knell for this long-standing tradition.

Music is another part of the show which dates back to the very earliest times. Local ensembles would often be engaged to entertain the crowds throughout the course of the day. In 1901 it was the Youlgreave United Prize Band which did the honours; Bakewell Free Church Band was another show-day regular. By 1910 organisers were aspiring to greater heights, with the 'famous band of the Yorkshire Hussars (Alexandra, Princess of Wales' Own)' taking top billing. The following year the Farmers' Club came up with a cunning way of laying on cheap entertainment by staging a band contest on the showground. Open to all amateur bands for an entrance fee of ten shillings, it was an innovative way of providing a whole programme of entertainment for less than the cost of the prize money, which totalled £18.

By the 1920s the attractions of a 'fun' element had evidently become apparent: one of the main events highlighted in show promotions of the time was children's mounted musical chairs, which attracted greater prominence on the front of the 1920 catalogue than the Band of the Queen's Own Hussars. There were also block tests, guessing the dead weight of a cow, sheep or pig, with tickets at around 6d. each and prizes of up to £1.

Exhibitions and demonstrations of crafts such as butter making and bee-keeping were introduced. Organisers also experimented with other popular activities: in 1926 whippet racing was added to the list. But the first moves towards the major centre-ring attractions we enjoy today came the following year. In 1928 the show featured a display of Highland dancing by the 1st Battalion Seaforth Highlanders, whose band was also performing that day. But that was only part of the entertainment. According to the official programme their parade was followed by a Grand Military Tournament starring officers of the Weedon Equitation School. Beginning with a thrilling activity ride designed to show off their feats of horsemanship, it also included a display of Arab tent pegging and the 'famous Cowboy Ride' – much talked about following its success at the recent Royal Tournament at Olympia.

This obviously went down well with show-goers because the event became a regular crowd-puller from then on. Over the next few years the Grand Military Display featured not only band music, but also a whole range of other skills. In 1929 the 5th Inniskillin Dragoon Guards performed a musical ride; the 1st Battalion Northumberland Fusiliers put on a display of physical training; and both regiments joined forces for a demonstration of mounted sports including push-ball and the old favourite musical chairs. In 1930 a parade and dancing by the Band of HM Scots Guards, Pipers and Drummers shared the spotlight with a field-gun display by the Royal Navy. This set the pattern for the next decade, with a succession of bands and regiments showing off the might of their military muscle in the centre ring.

Things changed slightly when the show was relaunched after the war. In 1946 troops were still regrouping in the wake of the conflict and were in no position to take time off to star at an agricultural show. The honours that year went to Foden's Motor Works Band, which lent a fitting tone to the after-noon's proceedings: its programme began with a 'Passing of the Regiments' medley by Winter and concluded with 'Hands Across the Sea', a collection of patriotic airs.

No other displays were included on that occasion, but by 1947 things were back on course with a display by the Royal Signals and in 1949 the military relation-ship was firmly cemented when star attractions were a musical ride by the Household Cavalry and music from the Band of the Royal Horse Guards.

The Armed Forces have continued to feature annually at the show, with the notable exception of 1992. That year the traditional band was given its marching orders when costs soared to a prohibitive £8,000 – equivalent to £80 per minute, according to officials of the time. But the troops were back on parade the following year after a string of complaints from disappointed visitors. Since then the military presence has been maintained and the Band of the Yorkshire Volunteers (TA) has filled the bill on a regular basis.

By the postwar years other organisations were also getting in on the centre-ring action. Groups invited to put on demonstrations included the High Peak Hounds, which first appeared around 1949 and are still a popular part of the show to this day.

Equestrian events were also enjoying a greater emphasis, with British Show Jumping Association classes taking over the main arena for the last part of the afternoon. This competition has gone from strength to strength: in 1971 it was officially designated an Area International Show Jumping Trials and since then it has attracted numerous international names.

Horse power was also behind the success of another new feature, the parade of heavy-horse turnouts, which earned its place among regulars in the main ring in 1963. This procession of magnificent beasts, plaited, beribboned and bedecked with gleaming brass and leather, had long been a winner with visitors and still rates as one of the surest crowd-pullers. Another regular favourite is the inter-county mounted games (formerly the Pony Club games), modern-day successor to the mounted musical chairs event which had first proved popular more than a century before. Teams of young riders are put through their paces in a series of challenges designed to test

The cattle make a fine show as they parade with the winners at the 1972 show. (SN)

Another original centrepiece was the tug-o'-war event, introduced in 1979. Site manager Mike Patterson also happened to be an England official judge for the sport and he was asked by secretary Ted Brownhill to look into the possibility of setting up a competition at Bakewell. Mike said:

The problem, as always, was that it had to be during the day, which was difficult for a sport which involved a lot of manual workers. There were about 300 teams in the country, but most couldn't get time off work.

In the end it was decided to hold the contest at around 6p.m. A weight limit of 100 stone was imposed, which meant sides featured eight men of around 12 stone, not heavyweight competitors. And they all weighed in before the contest, in a tent at the side of the ring, to ensure fair play. The event featured mostly teams from Derbyshire and neighbouring Staffordshire and took place in front of the grandstand: 'Spectators had a good view from there and they were safely out of the way, so you didn't get people with umbrellas poking members of their team... or the opposition!'

The move towards embracing activities other than those strictly associated with the farming industry began around 1956 when one of the main centre-ring attractions was a display by the Royal Corps of Signals Motor Cycle Team. While clearly a development of the show's well-established military links, it nonetheless set a new standard for the kind of breathtaking spectacles which are a crucial ingredient of any modern event.

Highlights in recent years have ranged from displays by moto-equestrian stunt riders and the White Helmets Motor Cycle Team to HM Prison guard dogs, and groups specialising in vaulting and Japanese dancing. There have been numerous special appearances too, which have served as crowd-pullers in their own right.

A helicopter display over the centre ring.

speed, skill and agility: from potato-picking races to straightforward obstacle courses.

Some of the most memorable arena displays have been created especially for Bakewell, such as the Derbyshire Young Farmers' cavalcade. The first such event took place in 1967 and is still remembered fondly by those who took part and others who watched from the grandstand. The cavalcade comprised a series of 48 tableaux representing each of the four seasons through the ages: from Stone-Age beginnings to a radio-controlled tractor of tomorrow, by way of Saxon ploughing, Georgian milkmaids, Victorian haymakers and steam-driven threshing-machines. 'It was wonderful,' recalls former show president Mary Daybell, one of the thousands who witnessed the event that day. 'The only thing that didn't go according to plan was the weather... it was followed by a terrible thunderstorm which put out all the electricity!'

So well enjoyed was the pageant that the Young Farmers were prevailed upon to put on a repeat performance in 1975 and then again in 1993, when it was a tribute to that year's president, Richard Morten. A Young Farmers stalwart, alongside wife Mary, he was one of those who took part in the original cavalcade.

Royal Marines give a demonstration of unarmed combat at the 1990 show. (DET)

Above: *High Peak Hounds give a demonstration at the 1977 show.* (SN)

Below: *The Moto-Equestrian Display Team.*

Left: *Miss World (Penny Plummer, from Australia) sits watching the main ring action with Mrs Matthew Longson and Brian Bakel at the 1969 show.*

Below: *The thrills and spills of the centre ring – an early visit from the White Helmets.* (McC)

Bottom: *Champions line up for the grand parade.* (DT)

In 1975 much excitement was caused by the attendance of 'Womble' Great Uncle Bulgaria, there to encourage a litter-free ground. Inanimate attractions over the years have ranged from veteran film star Chitty Chitty Bang Bang and 007's famous Saab turbo jet car to BP's 31,000-cubic-foot hot-air racing balloon.

Highlights at the 2001 show included the Mega Minis stunt-driving team, awesome strength and precision from the world-famous Welsh Axemen and displays by the Rockwood Dogs, father-daughter strongarm duo Tony Brutus and Amanda, and comedy slapstick act Tom and Tilly Turnip. Dropping in – literally – on the showground is always guaranteed to get everyone's attention and show-stoppers over the years have included the Toyota Aerobatic Display, the *Daily Express* Flying Crusaders women's parachutists, Ansells Skydivers and the Royal Marines freefall parachute and helicopter display team. 'It's caused some fun now and again,' remembers show director Brian Bakel:

One very wet year gallons of rainwater collected on top of the grandstand. When the helicopters hovered above the centre ring, the downdraught lifted the canopy and deposited the contents all over the people underneath.

Another year the watching crowds gasped in horror when a body apparently fell out of a helicopter taking part in a freefall parachute display... it turned out to be a dummy.

There is little chance of such a scare happening again; these days rigid health and safety legislation means this kind of display can no longer take place over a public arena. The law has also put paid to arguably the show's greatest centrepiece, for the time being at least. The Grand Parade of champions has been the focal point of every show from the very first back in 1819, as proud farmers showed off their prizewinning animals. Such was the importance attached to the parade that from 1911 a special notice appeared in the show catalogue – printed in red so that it stood out from other pages – instructing exhibitors that all cattle and horse winners were required to parade in the large ring. And there were dire consequences for anyone foolish enough to disobey. It warned: 'Exhibitors failing to comply with this notice will, at the discretion of the committee, forfeit any prize or prizes which may have been awarded to them.'

For years crowds gathered at 3p.m. each afternoon to enjoy the spectacle of huge bulls and Shire horses, magnificent rams and dainty goats, all proudly parading in their winners' rosettes around the centre ring. But after the 2001 foot-and-mouth epidemic, restrictions on livestock movement prevented cattle, sheep and goats from joining horses in the main arena. Determined not to be done out of their moment of glory, the stockmen began to stage their own miniparade in the livestock area while horses maintained the old tradition in the centre ring.

The future of the Grand Parade now hangs in the balance. While show-goers and exhibitors clamour for a return to the time-honoured spectacle, organisers admit that such a move would constitute a health-and-safety nightmare.

With regulations and legislation tightening their stranglehold all the time, the prospect of bringing bulls back to the centre ring is fraught with problems and looks increasingly unlikely. Perhaps the dawn of the new millennium in 2000 will go down in history as the year of the final Grand Parade.

Simply the best? The cattle judges will decide.

Shepherds give this Suffolk Tup a final trim before the judging. (DT)

❧ Eighteen ❧

Taking Stock

**SILCOCK'S,
The "Perfect" Feed**

For CATTLE, SHEEP, and PIG
Rearing, Milk Production and Fattening.
Ready for use in Cake, Nuts, and Meals.

Silcock's Calf Meal, "The Best Milk Substitute."

Experience with Silcock's Cake or Meal
is "The Best Test." —— TRY IT !

Local Agent : W. Harris, 79, Shaw Heath, Stockport.

Farming ain't what it used to be, as any good seasoned stockman will testify. Over the years the rose-tinted storybook image of corn sheaves and rustic barnyards has given way to the cold reality of high-tech agriculture. As time has marched on, so has technology and today's farmers are a hardy breed who know how to achieve the best from their land and their livestock. Today's Bakewell Show reflects that fact.

As humble beginnings go, it was pretty respectable. That first show, in 1819, attracted several dozen cattle, sheep, pigs and horses in 18 different classes. But few could have predicted back then the size and stature which the event would one day achieve. Today it is a landmark on the agricultural calendar, attracting over 6,000 entries in more than 700 classes, including several supreme championships and competitions for horses, donkeys, pigeons, poultry, rabbits, dogs, goats, cattle and sheep.

In the early days classes were fairly general. The only breeds specified were Longhorn and Shorthorn cattle, horses were defined merely as the 'draught' or the 'riding' kind, sheep as either Long- or Shortwool and pigs as large or small breed. That original livestock schedule has been gradually expanded to encompass the whole spectrum of farm animals.

Growth was rapid at first. By the second show the number of classes had jumped from 18 to 27 and in the third year that figure almost doubled to 50. But even then there was fluctuation as different competitions were introduced or discarded in a bid to keep pace with change.

By the time poultry made an appearance in 1857, Longhorn cattle had already been dropped because they were in decline. Specific breeds were starting to be defined: poultry that year included old varieties such as Dorkings, Brahmas and Spanish and the Derbyshire Redcap was added a year or two later. In 1879 – when rabbits and geese put in their first appearance – the poultry exhibition was hailed as the best to date, with a tremendous entry of Old English Game. Breed definitions were generally becoming more common: in 1884 three classes were allocated specifically for Shropshire sheep, now rare. But curiously, although the Shire Horse Society had begun to make its mark, Bakewell's catalogue continued to refer to 'horses of the draught kind'.

Some 70 years after it was founded, Bakewell Show was flourishing. Dogs were introduced in 1878 and a decade later entries for the show included 213 of them, as well as 50 cattle, 35 sheep, 126 horses, 15 pigs, 99 poultry, 225 pigeons, 51 rabbits and 9 cats.

New ideas were being tried all the time and a popular innovation at the turn of the century was the light-horse section, with its hunter, harness and Hackney competitions. It was as well there were fresh events to swell the programme: in 1902 pig classes fell victim to swine fever and two years later, inexplicably, both the dog and poultry sections were abandoned, remaining absent from the schedules for six years.

During this time, in 1903, Derbyshire Gritstone sheep made their first appearance under their old local name, Dales-o-Goyt. The breed reverted to its more common title from then on and still features as a major part of the show. In 1946 the breed society formally appointed Bakewell as its major exhibition and from then on has annually awarded four silver perpetual challenge cups to registered animals competing at the event.

Following the First World War, the show resumed in 1920 under its previous format, but the following year saw more innovations including a competition for Blue Albion cattle – a trend later taken up by other leading shows across the country. This new breed was a speciality of former show secretary William Clark, who was also involved in promoting Old English Blue Lupin pigs. The latter, a cross between a Large White boar and a Large Black sow, never caught on and did not feature at Bakewell, but the Blue Albion cattle classes remained until 1946 when they were replaced by the increasingly popular Channel Island varieties.

The postwar era was a progressive one for the show. Other 'firsts' included classes for Large White, Middle White and Gloucester Old Spot pigs – all introduced in 1923 (although the latter was dropped two years later) – and British Friesian cattle. Still popular today, these animals, with their distinctive black-and-white

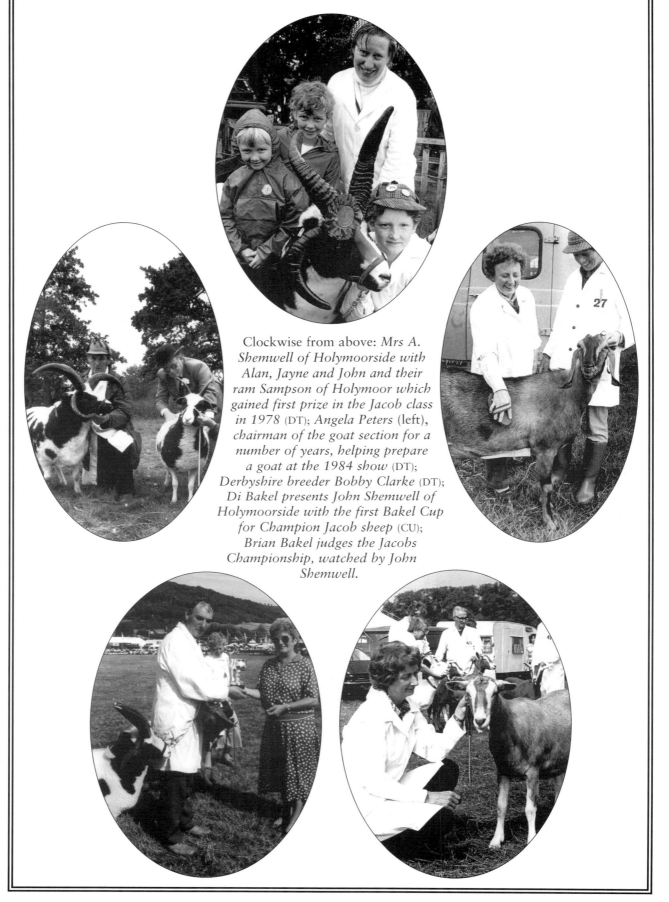

Clockwise from above: *Mrs A. Shemwell of Holymoorside with Alan, Jayne and John and their ram Sampson of Holymoor which gained first prize in the Jacob class in 1978* (DT); *Angela Peters* (left), *chairman of the goat section for a number of years, helping prepare a goat at the 1984 show* (DT); *Derbyshire breeder Bobby Clarke* (DT); *Di Bakel presents John Shemwell of Holymoorside with the first Bakel Cup for Champion Jacob sheep* (CU); *Brian Bakel judges the Jacobs Championship, watched by John Shemwell.*

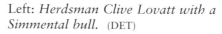

Left: *Herdsman Clive Lovatt with a Simmental bull.* (DET)

Below: *It's bath time for this Charolais at the 1974 show.*

Bottom right: *Bill McClimond with Chechnia, a Charolais cow owned by E. Dodd, at the 1974 show.* (SN)

Background image: *Mr J.C. Peat and his daughter Rosemary, both of Eckington Hall Farm, with their Jersey cows which gained first prize at the 1978 show.* (DT)

markings, first appeared in 1926 when there were entries from six exhibitors, three of them acknowledged local pioneers of the breed: Mr Frank Gilbert of Chellaston, Messrs E. and R. Willetts of Chaddesden and Messrs Smedley's Hydro Co. of Matlock.

Around this time the Ministry of Agriculture and Fisheries launched an innovative livestock improvement scheme, designed to encourage top-quality breeding by paying premiums to farmers keeping high-class-graded bulls. Bakewell acknowledged the move in 1921 by inaugurating a class for these so-called 'scheme' bulls; the first winner was a Dairy Shorthorn named Airman, exhibited by Mr J.E. Mycock of Flagg. Later more classes were also incorporated for the progeny of these animals.

Classification expanded again over the next few years as more new breeds were added, including Wessex Saddleback pigs. But undoubtedly the most fiercely-fought competition of the show was for Dairy Shorthorn cattle, the pre-eminent breed at the time. There were so many would-be exhibitors that organisers had to lay on 16 classes, requiring three separate judges for the bulls, cows and heifers, to adjudicate for more than 180 animals.

The 1930s marked another period of change for Bakewell. New on the schedule at that time were classes for Jersey cattle, the Large Black pig and Suffolk, Oxford, Hampshire and Shropshire sheep. In 1934 Ayrshire cattle also made their first appearance, although the breed was far from new, having been introduced to Derbyshire nearly a century before. This breed continues to feature on the schedule, with classes for cows, heifers and heifers in calf – which accounts for the celebration of a happy event on the showground in 1959. Allestree Lady Emma, an Ayrshire heifer, was born during the show and sealed her link with the event three years later when she was a winner in her own right, as one of a pair of heifers in calf.

Promotion of good practice and quality herds has always been a priority for the society and with this in mind it agreed to sponsor a Young Farmers' calf-rearing class in 1938. Competitors, all from the recently-formed Young Farmers' Clubs at Bakewell, Matlock and Hope Valley, were challenged to rear a heifer calf and keep a diary of its progress. They had to record all relevant details, from age and size of the animal to the quantity and cost of feed, and exhibit it on show day.

The competition was judged by Professor H.G. Robinson, principal of the Midland Agricultural College, who awarded first prize of £2 to T.G. Mosley

A Middle White champ at the 1974 show.

of Highfield Farm, Ashford, second (£1.10.s) to K.O. Wigley of Moorside Farm, Tansley, and third (£1) to Barbara Bowler of Ewe Close Farm, Bakewell.

The Young Farmers continue to play an important part in Bakewell Show with calf classes, which carry their own challenge trophies and supreme championship, and their own stock-judging competition. Continuity was broken again during the Second World War, but in 1946 the show took up where it had left off. Dairy Shorthorn classes remained popular but there was increased competition from other breeds, with the notable introduction of Guernseys in place of Blue Albions. Over the next few years Herefords, Red Polls, Dexters and Aberdeen Angus were also added to the cattle schedule.

In the pig section the Essex and Landrace breeds made an appearance, the latter a high-quality bacon pig introduced from Sweden and destined to play a major part in British bacon production. Conversely, sheep classes were slimmed down to just three: Derbyshire Gritstone, any other pure breed, and crossbred animals.

Around this time dramatic changes occurred in the poultry classes, with purebred fowl very much on the decline. Rhode Island Red, Brown Leghorn and Light Sussex were among the breeds used in commercial crosses which became very popular for a time. They were eventually usurped by the modern hybrids and broiler chickens – all of which left the traditional breeds in grave danger of extinction. Frank Clarke, chairman of the small livestock committee for more than 20 years, said:

Farmers who continued to exhibit these breeds at Bakewell and many similar shows should be credited for their foresight and enthusiasm in keeping the stock of the old breeds alive, and preserving valuable genetic material for possible future use...

In 1946 the poultry section recorded 221 entries in 42 classes, with breeds including Old English Game, Indian Game, Wyandotte, Leghorn, Rhode Island Red, Orpington, Ancona and the Derbyshire Redcap as well as classes for bantams and eggs. These were expanded in the 1950s with the inclusion of Gold and Silver Selright, Belgian and Pekin. All of these have since been dropped, but the success of the competition has gone from strength to strength.

Today the record numbers of 1946 have almost trebled. In 2002 there were 642 entries in 148 classes,

This image: *Poultry judges in action.*

Left: *Pigeons on display.*

with the addition of modern breeds including the Silkie, Minorca, Welsummer, Wyandotte, White Crested and Frizzle Feathered Poland, Sussex, Australorp and New Hampshire Red, as well as classes for waterfowl and pigeons.

Pigeon classes play a comparatively small part in the show because Bakewell's regular August slot is the wrong time of year for fanciers: many older birds are moulting and younger ones are not yet sufficiently grown. However, entries have increased steadily, from 54 in 1946 to 111 in 2002, including classes for racing pigeons and fancy varieties.

The pigeon and poultry show is recognised as one of the best on the circuit and in 1987 it was awarded regional-championship status by the official Poultry Club of Great Britain – a designation which carries with it a number of breed-club awards and special trophies as well as considerable prestige.

Goats were introduced for the first time in 1953 and quickly became an established part of the show. The innovation proved as popular with exhibitors as it did with show-goers, according to goat steward Angela Peters, who was in charge of the section for more than a decade:

All exhibitors comment on the lovely setting and now we're based in the agricultural centre they talk wistfully of our days on the tranquil riverbank. A marquee next to the river can quickly turn into a quagmire in wet weather – which is a big problem when you're trying to unload equipment and keep your animals clean at the same time. On the other hand, boiling hot weather under canvas can be overpowering. I remember having to use wet towels to cool the goats down!

Leading exhibitors in the early days, according to steward Winifred King, were mainly women 'who seemed to have plenty of time and money to spare.' She recalled:

Some were in the happy position of being accompanied to the show by their driver-

cum-stockman who undertook most of the chores of showing. It was not unusual to see the odd silver coffee pot, silver spoons and china cups amidst the straw of the exhibitors' tent.

The most successful goat exhibitor of her time was Miss Mostyn-Owen, whose champion Mostyn Daphne was named best in show for five successive years between 1962–66. The section reached its peak in 1979 with a record 288 entries. Since then the British Goat Society has clamped down on its rules and regulations and exhibitor numbers have slumped on a nationwide basis. But the show remains popular with both breeders and visitors. In 2002 the 26 classes attracted well over 100 entries.

The 1960s brought little change for the show but signalled the beginning of the end for pig classes. Finances were tight and, despite a drive to boost income and cut expenditure, new ways had to be found to make economies. The weight of the axe fell on the pig schedule and the difficult decision was taken to delete the Middle White, Wessex Saddleback, Essex and latterly the Large White breed too, leaving only Landrace classes.

In 1973 even these had to be cancelled after yet another outbreak of swine fever and the following year, when swine vesicular disease struck, the pig section was scrapped altogether. The loss was mourned by those who had helped to run it over the years, but the move reflected farming trends of the time. As large-scale commercial production took over from traditional methods, fewer farmers were keeping pigs. Purebred British herds were on the decline and it was simply no longer viable to farm the old-fashioned breeds. Pig classes have not been included since then, but pigs can be found on the showground today as part of the rare breeds exhibition, along with traditional varieties of sheep and cattle which are no longer commonly farmed.

The '70s heralded a new era for livestock classes, with the introduction in 1971 of Charolais beef cattle, the first of many 'exotic' breeds which were popular at

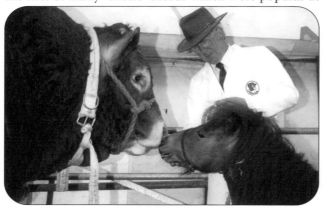

D'arcy the bull and Lulu the Shetland pony – he wouldn't come to the show without her – and their owner Les Wilson. (DET)

Right: *J.J. Brocklehurst parades his champion Derbyshire Gritstone sheep.*

the time. This was followed three years later by the addition of Simmental beef cattle and Jacob sheep.

Breeds continue to come and go, like Hampshire sheep, which were popular for a time, and British Charollais sheep, which are a fairly recent addition. Others dropped in more recent years have included Dexter, Guernsey and Red Poll cattle while Holstein, Belgian Blue, Highland and Limousin classes have all been added – the latter breed renowned in Bakewell circles for its sentimentality. Champion Limousin bull D'arcy made headlines in 1991, not for his vast stature or winning form, but because he refused to co-operate with owner Les Wilson of Westwood unless long-standing fieldmate Lulu, a 26in miniature Shetland pony, was allowed to share his pen.

Rabbits, originally introduced in 1879, disappeared from the show towards the late 1800s but they were reintroduced almost exactly a century after their first appearance. In 1976 chief steward Ken Watts took charge of 20 classes for fancy breeds, such as Dutch and English Dwarfs, and 18 fur (long-haired) and rex (short-haired) classes for varieties such as Satins, Chinchilla, Havanas and Rex. Interest has picked up considerably since then and in 2002 there were 52 fancy classes and another 61 for fur and rex animals.

Ken Watts and his wife Viv remained at the helm for more than 20 years, finally stepping down from stewarding duties after the 2002 show. But their contribution has established the rabbit section as a regular part of Bakewell and a firm favourite with visitors. It comes as no surprise to the couple – showing rabbits is both a pleasure and a serious business as far as they are concerned. Between them, Ken and Viv have been breeding and exhibiting rabbits for around 50 years. They keep 30 animals at any one time, feeding them a diet of pellets, supplemented with titbits of carrots, dandelions, toasted bread and Weetabix. Show-day preparations include a thorough brushing, a rub down with a moist cloth and a polish with a piece of velvet or silk, but there is no sentimentality attached to rabbit breeding. Viv is reported as saying: 'It's winners or dinners in this household!'

On The Move

Nineteen

Long queues of traffic tailing back along Thirteen Bends Road are as synonymous with Bakewell Show as wet weather and prize bulls. Not that the event actually brings the Peak District grinding to a halt on an annual basis, it's just one of those legends which has grown up over the years and improved with the telling. When the show first began, of course, the phrase 'traffic chaos' had never been invented. A farmer no doubt rode to the gathering on his workaday mare, took the family along in the pony trap or simply walked across the fields.

But transport – or rather the lack of it – caused problems even then. The show soon became an important occasion on the countryman's calendar but the distance to Bakewell made it impossible for many would-be visitors to join in the fun. In 1840 the society took the unusual step of moving the event, flock, stock and barrel, to Alfreton Park so that east Derbyshire folk could have their first chance to attend.

Bakewell's growing popularity brought in entries from a wider region each year and its appeal increased still further with the advent of livestock transport. By 1880 farmers were bringing their cattle, sheep and pigs from all across the county and beyond, with apparently no ill effects – records show that a herd of Shorthorn cattle belonging to one Mr T.H. Oakes of Riddings carried off 11 first prizes that year, as well as five seconds and a third.

The railways played an increasingly important role over the next few decades, putting the show within easy reach of town folk and city dwellers for miles around. It was a popular day out for jaded workers and their families, keen to escape from the dirt and grime of urban living and soak up the fresh air and freedom of the countryside for a few hours. In 1898 the local press reported that the Midland Railway Company put on 100 extra coaches for the occasion and had their busiest day ever at Bakewell Station.

By the turn of the century the show relied on the railways to bring in the vast majority of its spectators. In the 1930s, after the disruptions of the Great War, late trains were advertised on show day each year, leaving Bakewell at around 9p.m. and dropping off passengers at all stations en route to Manchester. The burgeoning popularity of the motor car stepped up competition for British Railways, which strove to attract more passengers by laying on extra services for big events. In the 1950s special trains were advertised for show-goers from as far afield as Derby, Nottingham, Rotherham, Wolverhampton, Birmingham, Leicester and Manchester, with cheap day-return tickets available within a 60-mile radius of the showground. 'Travel in rail comfort,' proclaimed the announcements – and they did. In 1958 an astonishing 2,229 passengers were reportedly delivered to Bakewell Station by seven early-morning specials, and

Temporary Bailey bridge over the River Wye, first erected for the 1947 show. (McC)

another 22 trains left between 3:30–9p.m., taking them all home again. Such was the demand for public transport that the London St Pancras to Manchester express made a rare stop in Bakewell on the day before the show.

But by this time the motor vehicle had begun to take over as the most convenient method of travel for many people and that brought a whole new set of problems for Bakewell. Tucked away in the heart of the picturesque Peak District, the town was no stranger to tourism, but its roads had not been designed to cope which such an influx of traffic on one day. Narrow country lanes became quickly choked in all directions and even the main A6 became congested as cattle trucks, horseboxes and carloads of visitors all headed for the show.

As early as 1954 local papers reported that hold-ups on the road from Baslow were so bad that it took around 40 minutes to cover the final mile or two. Some people simply gave up, parked their cars at the roadside and walked the last stretch to the show-ground. Coaches and buses helped to ease the problem; the show was a favourite destination for tour operators and special day-trips were laid on by companies for miles around. In fact coach operators made such an important contribution to ticket sales over the years that many of them were appointed as official agents. These still include companies as far away as Blackburn in Lancashire, Congleton in Cheshire, Radford in Nottinghamshire, Swinton in Yorkshire and Ashton-under-Lyne.

Of course, this reliance on public transport opened up another area of potential hazard. Attendance at the 1957 show was severely threatened by the prospect of a bus strike; thankfully it was called off in the nick of time. And in 1965 celebrations of a near-record entry in the pigeon and poultry section were dampened by a dire warning from manager Mr R. Evans: 'Almost 75 per cent of our entries come by rail and with the continuous closure of stations, and higher rail charges, the future of this particular show is uncertain,' he said. 'I don't think it will close completely, but this hurdle will have to be met.' It was no idle threat. Three years later Bakewell had fallen victim to the Beeching axe and was left without an operational railway. As far as the show was concerned, the pigeons and poultry suffered most as a result of this blow because they had to be taken off the train at Matlock and loaded onto lorries for the remaining eight miles of the journey. On the other hand it meant that their classes attracted more local breeders. It also meant an inevitable increase in road traffic. Some of the congestion problems had already been ironed out, such as a single-span crossing over the River Wye which had been a regular bottle-neck in the past but was replaced by a two-way traffic Bailey bridge.

Organisers were geared up to deal with the extra cars and, in the event, the loss of rail services caused less disruption than anticipated. Inspector F. Woodings of Bakewell Police told the *Derbyshire Times* newspaper:

Things have gone extremely smoothly and we'll be happy if they continue like this until the show is over. But seeing as there are no trains we are standing by to handle more coaches from Derby, Sheffield and Nottingham.

That set the pattern for the next decade or so and very little changed during the '70s. Local media reports habitually made much of the long tailbacks and lengthy delays for anyone trying to reach the show-ground; Bakewell's name became tainted by the joint scourges of wet weather and traffic problems. It was a perpetual headache for organisers, who were powerless to prevent the steady build-up as show-goers headed for the ground – and even less influential when it came to contributory factors beyond their control.

In 1990 tempers boiled over after roadworks, a fallen tree and a minor accident combined to cause chaos on the roads. By 10:30a.m. the A619 had come to a standstill and a seven-mile queue was waiting impatiently to get into Bakewell. Little of it was down to the show, but it got the blame anyway.

Organisers, still smarting from the unjust criticism, rounded on Derbyshire County Council three years later when the A621 Baslow Road was closed in advance of show day for three months of carriageway repairs. The move was condemned by irate show secretary Ted Brownhill as 'total, utter and complete incompetence'. It was calculated to cause outrage because by that time – despite regular ill-informed claims to the contrary – the traffic problems were largely under control. Two major innovations were responsible for this major leap forward: a new park-and-ride scheme and the use of the Monsal Trail.

Moves to relieve the effects of the annual show snarl-up gathered pace in 1984 when the committee joined forces with the Peak National Park Board and local bus operators to try to find a solution. The suggestion was made that the old Buxton to Matlock railway line – now used as a path for walkers and cyclists – should be employed as a shortcut for buses to ferry passengers to and from the showground. Various trackbed improvements were needed before the plan could be put into action. Proposals to lower part of the pathway, so double-deckers could negotiate an overhead bridge, were eventually dropped and the route was authorised for use by single-deck buses only.

Walkers and cyclists were banned from the Monsal Trail for the two show days.

The experiment proved a roaring success. The last passenger train had left Hassop Station in 1927, but more than half a century later it was back in use with a vengeance. During that first year several hundred people boarded buses at Hassop for the free ten-minute journey to Bakewell. Many service buses were re-routed down the trail, as well as minibuses specially laid on for the purpose. One operator reported: 'It was the first time we had run to schedule on a show day!'

These days stewards have the service down to a fine art and thousands of visitors annually beat the bottle-necks by taking advantage of the park-and-ride system. There are now three sites with space for more than 1,000 cars – two are located near Hassop round-about, at Hassop Station Farm and the nearby Station Sidings, while a third is based at Pineapple Farm on the Baslow side of Thirteen Bends Road.

The traffic jams of yesteryear are little more than a distant memory now, although people are still inclined to complain at the first hint of a hold-up. These days show congestion is usually due either to accidents or just plain stupidity. Take the first day of the show in 1998 for example. More than 3,000 angry motorists were left fuming after a lorry driver decided to turn his low loader around in fields off the A6. Because of torrential rain earlier in the week the field, a car park for visitors' vehicles, was soft and the ground was quickly churned into a quagmire. Cars had to be re-directed to alternative parking and metal tracking was brought in so that the boggy field could be used the following day. 'Ten or twelve acres of car parking had been rendered unusable by one careless person,' said show official Robin Rhodes. 'Obviously it has spoilt the day for a great deal of people, which we regret, but it was not our doing. In future metal tracking will always be provided.'

So visitors to future shows can rest assured that everything possible is being done to ensure their journey is as swift, smooth and trouble-free as possible. But if all else fails, perhaps they should follow the lead of one young equestrienne. She found her horsebox trapped in a line of stationary traffic en route to the showground and, with less than an hour to go before her event, feared she would not make it in time. Leaning out of the window, she attracted the attention of a nearby police officer and explained her predicament. He came up with the perfect solution. While the girl nipped in the back of the vehicle and changed into her riding gear, he unloaded her horse from the trailer. Then he took her place behind the wheel of the van and she saddled up, mounted and rode off into the sunset.

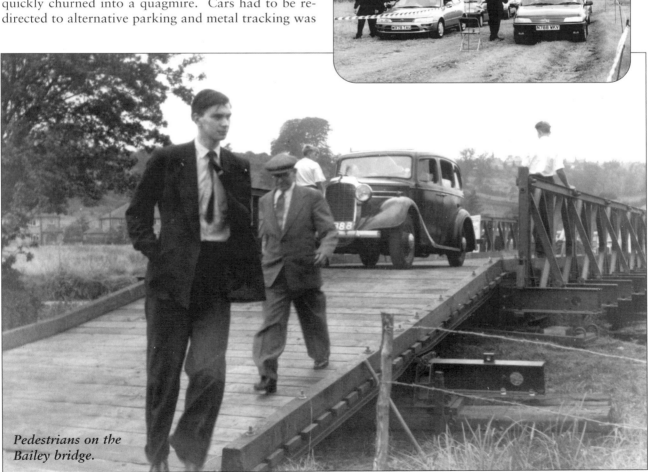

Traffic control.

Pedestrians on the Bailey bridge.

Left: *The bull who went for an unscheduled run around the centre ring.* (ROD LEACH)

Main: *Parachutists can be blown off course.*

Twenty

Animal Crackers

Never work with animals or children, goes the old adage... hardly an option where Bakewell Show is concerned, but for seasoned stalwarts the hazard is simply part of the fun. Animals have always been the pivotal focus of the show and years of experience have honed the preparations for their arrival into an operation of military precision. The prospect of gathering together well over 7,000 livestock on 36 acres of land, a space little larger than the average municipal park, demands a mammoth feat of organisation.

For the most part the animals are surprisingly well behaved. The majority, after all, have been rounded up and enticed into the unfamiliar surroundings of livestock wagons or horseboxes, driven over considerable distances and then fussed over, groomed, primped and preened to ensure they look their best. Some, particularly dogs and horses, are veterans of the show circuit and have grown accustomed to the demands of the judges (to say nothing of their proud owners). But they are, after all, just ordinary animals and their unpredictability has occasionally provided more of a spectacle than intended, sometimes with dramatic consequences. Take the infamous 'mad elephant incident' which rocked Bakewell in 1905 and has gone down in the annals of show history, even though it did not happen during the event itself. Crowds had flocked to the showground on 25 May to see Lord John Sanger's circus with its star attraction, a troupe of performing elephants. Disaster struck half way through the performance as the Sangers acrobatic team prepared for the highlight of their act, leaping between ladders tied to the elephants' backs.

As one of the beasts, a 65-year-old male named Philis, lumbered into the ring he suddenly turned on his keeper, Frank Bailey. The audience watched in horror as the keeper was knocked to the ground and horrified shrieks broke out as Philis then knelt on him. Attendants hurried to lead the elephant out of the big top, but the terror was not over. A newspaper report at the time painted a frightening picture of events:

The sides of the tent began to sway ominously and the head and trunk of the animal, tearing down the canvas, was thrust through the aperture, notwithstanding the attempts of keepers with pronged forks to bar its progress.

Pandemonium ensued as onlookers stampeded for the exits, the elephant rampaged and circus manager George Sanger Coleman was badly mauled as he tried to intervene. He and Frank Bailey were both carried off for treatment – Bailey to the new Union Infirmary and Coleman, strangely, to the Rutland Arms Hotel.

Witnesses are divided over exactly what happened next. Some say a unit of Derbyshire Yeomanry, camping at nearby Chatsworth, was called in; others claim Sergeant Instructor Sheppard of the Bakewell Volunteer Company, Sherwood Foresters, came to the rescue with the help of audience members. He, apparently, had served ten years in India and 'knew the ways of elephants and how to deal with them under such circumstances.' The top priority was to stop the maddened beast before anyone else was seriously hurt. Keepers, armed with ropes, chains and pulley blocks, tried to restrain him but were hampered by crowds of onlookers who were riveted to the spectacle. The *Derbyshire Times* reported:

Bakewell has never been more excited. The danger was all the greater as, notwithstanding the utmost efforts of the police and the show people to secure the animal, thousands of people were assembled all round, watching the proceedings – a dangerous curiosity indeed, should the animal have broken loose, though many took the precaution of watching from the other side of a wall.

The elephant was finally captured and brought to his knees. The shooting party took aim and Philis was shot dead before a thousand-strong crowd of excited witnesses: reportedly the only elephant to be killed in Britain.

Attempts were made to continue the performance, but at a quarter-past nine it was finally abandoned: 'The turns were too tame after a man had been knelt upon by an elephant and had been carried away on a stretcher. There was no relish for many in the everyday circus item,' said the newspaper. The circus moved off to Buxton early next morning, leaving behind the huge carcass which measured 17 feet from trunk to tail, stood nearly ten feet tall and weighed around four tons. It lay on the showground for several days while the authorities pondered the problem of how to dispose of a slaughtered elephant.

Left: *The dead elephant is winched onto a wagon.*

Below: *Souvenir hunters pose on the dead beast.*

Cubes of skin and even larger parts were cut off as souvenirs before it was finally removed, using a crane and horses, to the town tip at Greenhills. It is said that at least five people claim to have umbrella stands made from the feet of that elephant!

The year 1905 was a dramatic one for Bakewell – two more disasters involving animals happened just months later, on show day itself. The first involved a bull: a breed with a well-deserved reputation for unpredictability and which, even in capable hands, can prove bad tempered. A young handler by the name of Fisher, from Wingerworth in Chesterfield, was leading a bull from its pen into the ring. The animal had grown increasingly irritable as the time approached for its class to be judged. Finally roused to anger as it was herded into place in the line-up, it charged at its handler and gored him so badly that the lad had to be rushed to hospital with serious internal injuries.

Hardly had the crowd recovered its equilibrium when disaster struck again, although this time it was the animal that came off worst. Triumph turned to tragedy when a valuable Southdown ram, which had just won its class, was being loaded for the homeward journey at Bakewell railway station. It slipped, breaking a hind leg so badly that it had to be slaughtered by local butcher Mr A.J. Critchlow.

Arguably the most serious disaster – it proved fatal – came a few years later, in 1911, and was again linked to the show by folklore rather than fact. It actually happened on Easter Monday, when Shire stallions were traditionally paraded through the streets of Bakewell, attracting large crowds of spectators. During the parade, groom Albert Strang, of Whittington in Chesterfield, stumbled and collided with the horse in front. It instinctively kicked out with its powerful hind legs, striking Strang on the head, sending him flying and fracturing his skull in the process. He never recovered – and nor did the parade. From then on it was taken off the streets and held in the relative safety of a local field.

More recently, in 1976, tragedy struck a family from Brighton who were visiting Bakewell Show as part of their summer holiday. An hour after arriving at the event their estate car burst into flames in the car park, trapping their six-month-old labrador puppy inside. Officials battled to push nearby cars out of the way, to stop the fire spreading, but the dog died in the blaze.

The show made headlines in 1987 following a drama on the big wheel in the children's fairground. Eleven-year-old Candice Smith of Whaley Bridge fell 15 feet but escaped with cuts and bruises after being tipped out mid-ride. Step-brother Tony, eight, clung on by his fingertips until he could be rescued. Mum Christine Smith looked on, horrified, as events unfolded. She told the *Sheffield Star*:

As they came over the top of the ride the door came open and Candy was flung out. She was hanging on by her arms but couldn't hold on any longer and fell on to metal bars underneath.

The ride's owner was later ordered by health-and-safety officials to modify the locking system.

Not all mishaps were so dramatic, of course. Frank Clarke, who has been showing pigeons since he was a boy, recalls many incidents during the 20 years since he became chairman of the small livestock committee. Escapees are a regular hazard for him, with up to 800 pigeons, poultry and rabbits on site. One judge got more than he bargained for when a Derbyshire Redcap fowl – known for being flighty, nervous and very quick – flew between his legs as he began his examination. The judge made a grab but the bird kept going, leaving him with a handful of feathers... and a very red face. And a wayward pigeon ruffled a few feathers after it escaped into the marquee and eluded all attempts at recapture. Stewards were alerted to close all exits, but the bird flew high up into the top of the tent and perched on an electricity cable. Frank explained:

The problem was how to get him down. Someone suggested calling the fire brigade and they turned up with a ladder. But every time they approached the pigeon, it moved a bit further away. Eventually they came up with the idea of getting a landing net from Fisherman's Walk. One of the firemen was despatched to fetch it and eventually managed to climb up and net the bird, to great cheers and applause from the crowd gathered below!

Live television interviews are like a red rag to the proverbial bull – or in this case, a real one. In 1996 YTV presenter Alan Hardwick was deep in conversation with the proud owner of the show's champion bull when, across the other side of the centre ring, the military band struck up. The animal apparently took a liking to the rousing music and began to toss its head and dance around to the beat. The poor farmer struggled unsuccessfully to control over a tonne of prime British beef while Alan Hardwick struggled manfully to maintain his composure.

Show organisers have long been aware of the potential hazard posed by bulls. In 1982 they were left out of the Grand Parade altogether because the committee considered them too temperamental. The move triggered a deluge of complaints from farmers, but was vindicated to some extent the following year after the bulls were reinstated. An 11cwt Charolais champion broke free in the centre ring and bolted across the arena, dragging 22-year-old handler Peter Hawksworth with it. The beast was caught by another farmer and it took six men to calm it and lash it to a post. Meanwhile Peter needed hospital treatment for shock and bruising. Owner Ernest Hawksworth of Ashover was quoted in the *Sheffield Morning Telegraph* – under the headline 'Beserk bull top of class' – as saying: 'It must have been the hubbub of the crowd and the blare of the loudspeakers that did it.'

Humans can be every bit as troublesome as livestock, of course, particularly when the pressure is on and the efforts of 363 days' careful planning are about to come to fruition. In 1979 there was an eve-of-show panic when the horticulture marquee and a wooden toilet block were demolished by an eight-year-old 'joyrider'. She had been playing in the front seat of her mum's car when the Marina suddenly lurched forward and she found herself careering across the showground in a mass of torn canvas and splintered wood. The fruit and flower display stands were quickly repaired and officials ordered an emergency caravan of luxury replacement loos. Even so, they were nearly caught short when it was discovered at the last minute that no one had remembered to plumb in the water supply.

A trade stand collapsed in 1965 but for very different reasons. Resourceful visitors had decided to use the unoccupied stall as a platform to give them a grandstand view of the centre ring. Unfortunately it concertinaed under their weight and sent woodwork flying in all directions, injuring neighbouring stall-holder Eric Smith, MD of Gervase Smith and Sons.

But impending disaster was averted in 1993 when, in the nick of time, police controlling the Haddon Road car park spotted a vehicle travelling the wrong way around the showground's one-way traffic system. The lone Austin was stopped as it wove its way in and out of oncoming vehicles and officers were astonished to find its occupants were four Chinese men – trying to find their way to Manchester Airport!

Public humiliation is an occupational hazard for the professional performer and with so many involved in the show over the years, it is inevitable that one or two have met their downfall. Many centre-ring attractions hinge on split-second timing and breath-taking precision, which is awe-inspiring when everything goes according to plan. But when it doesn't the results can be catastrophic – not least to the victim's ego.

Fortunately the consequences were not serious in 1959 when one of the riders in the Royal Corps of Signals came to grief during a motorcycle display. He crashed his machine during an intricate stunt but escaped with minor injuries and bruised pride.

In 1987 one of the normally impeccably behaved mounts of the Household Cavalry disgraced itself by throwing its rider in the middle of the team's star performance. The arena display was just reaching its climax when the horse reared up and unceremoniously deposited the guard on his pristinely uniformed rear end in the mud. Not only did he suffer the indignity of having to hastily remount, but also had to stump up for the regiment's traditional 'punishment': a round of drinks for his 29 jeering colleagues.

Army parachutist Alan Cotterill found himself heading for trouble when he was blown off course during a display by the 63 Parachute Squadron in 1973. He did his best to correct his position as he drifted groundwards, but landed well off target – on top of a Ford Capri owned by show-goer Henry Taylor of Brook Farm, Belper.

Lumberjack Bill Huaki, one of the world-famous Welsh Axemen who starred in the 2001 show, had only himself to blame when he ended up in Chesterfield Royal Hospital to have 30 stitches in his leg. The axe wielder had been demonstrating his strength and precision in the horizontal chop – hacking through a log beneath his feet – when he suffered a momentary lapse in concentration, missed his balance and swung the axe into his shin. Luck, and a specially made pair of kevlar trousers, saved serious injury but the incident lent an extra thrill to the centre-ring attractions.

Bakewell Show has always been a rich hunting-ground for news hounds, but in 1989 an outbreak of food poisoning attracted the kind of publicity that any large-scale event can do without. One woman was taken to hospital and more than 100 visitors – including director John Smallman – were stricken by what was at first thought to be a sickness bug. Subsequent tests revealed that prawn cocktails and turkey, served in the members' enclosure, were to blame.

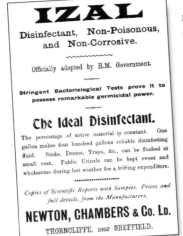

Rumours of another mystery illness were sparked after an incident involving young majorettes all taking part in a baton-twirling display. More than a dozen of them collapsed over the course of the afternoon and great controversy erupted as a variety of theories were suggested and then explored. After weeks of deliberation, not to mention several similar incidents elsewhere, the phenomenon was put down to the effects of mass hysteria.

Problems involving the elements have been well charted at the show but it was the wind, rather than the usual sun or rain, which played havoc in 1963. Gusts lifted the canvas in the dog tent, sending a tent pole crashing to the ground or, more exactly, on to the head of unsuspecting Glossop woman Margaret Platt. An ambulance was summoned and Mrs Platt was hurried to the showground first-aid tent for treatment. She later told the *Derbyshire Times*: 'We always come to Bakewell Show but this is the first time I've been driven through with bells ringing!' More weather problems took their toll in 1993 when, after weeks of heavy rain, the resulting quagmire added to traffic chaos on show day and caused a string of problems on the boggy showground. A refrigerated van, delivering a tonne of ice from Durham, skidded in the mud as its driver edged alongside the River Wye and slid down the bank, ending up axle-deep in sludge. 'I was just driving in slowly when the van slid across on the soft bank,' said driver Les Sams. 'It crossed my mind as we started to slide that we might end up in the river.' The van's engine was left running to stop the ice from melting and teams of waitresses ferried bucketloads of ice to the bar, so show-goers were not consigned to drinking warm champagne. But Mr Sams had to wait until the end of the day before a tractor could reach the van to tow it out of the mud.

Troublemakers have rarely been a problem on the showground, but gaining access to it is another matter entirely. Organisers were alerted one year when word spread of a scam being run by opportunists in pubs around the town. In those days visitors leaving the showground could have a coloured stamp printed on the back of their hand to allow them re-entry. Racketeers were ascertaining the colour and design of the stamp, then selling copies at a fraction of the admission price to late arrivals. That particular practice has since been scuppered by the use of security armbands.

In days before the site was reorganised, some unscrupulous visitors evaded paying the entry charge by wading across the River Wye. It was a popular way to sneak into the show on a hot day, but strictly for hardline swindlers when the river was swollen, fast-flowing and freezing cold. One ticket-dodger is reputed to have got his come-uppance after peeling off his shoes and socks to paddle across, and slashing his foot on a submerged bottle in the process. It is said he was stitched up by the resident vet – without the benefit of an anaesthetic!

Majorettes perform in the centre ring.

Twenty-One

A Growing Tradition

The current preoccupation with Alan Titchmarsh, 'Ground Force' and anything that involves decking or water features is a symptom of the nation's fascination with gardens. But the phenomenon is hardly new – and from the time when ordinary people first began to 'grow their own', Bakewell Show has provided an arena in which they could show off their prize fruit, veg and flowers.

The show comes in August, which is perfect for those specialising in gladioli or sweet peas, but a trifle early for the veg growers. The best onion ever exhibited at Bakewell was reportedly around 8lb, but by September 11lb whoppers are not uncommon and leeks are at their best with towering six-foot flags and barrels some five inches around.

In the early days the produce classes were strictly farm-based. As early as 1821 a special silver vase, worth 30 guineas, was awarded by the Board of Agriculture for the best-cultivated farm. Later classes were introduced for turnips and cabbages drawn from a crop of not less than half an acre. There was even a special class for the best 20 roots of common turnips from a crop not less than two acres grown with Taylor's manures – sponsored, surprise surprise, by Messrs W. and H. Taylor.

But as the century progressed, gardening became increasingly popular. Once an occupation confined to those who worked in and around the big houses, it gradually became a pastime for the masses. By 1898 the district was swamped with horticultural events and flower shows. The Bakewell Horticultural and Industrial Society was well-enough established but found itself in financial difficulties as a result of all the competition. The obvious answer, members decided, was to merge with the much stronger Agricultural Society in order to ensure the group's survival. The farmers were not so keen on this idea and a number of

These two small visitors are tempted by the gooseberries.

them raised objections. A meeting was called to thrash out the proposal and a lengthy discussion ensued over the various merits and drawbacks of the plan. Eventually the dissenters capitulated and it was agreed that a horticultural exhibition would be included in the annual show – but on a trial basis, for one year only.

The horticulture show added a new dimension to the popular event, proved an immediate success and has been an integral part of the society and its work ever since. By the time the show broke off during the First World War, many local people were regularly taking part in the annual competitions, entering their biggest cabbages, their rosiest apples and the most perfect blooms they could grow in their gardens.

When the show resumed after the war, one of the most popular new features was an exhibition by the County Council's Agricultural Education Department, a forerunner in some respects of today's horticultural exhibition. The display featured various skills of domestic farm life, including bee-keeping, and as local newspapers reported: 'It was thronged with spectators all day.' These days show-goers can study honey production close up at a display which includes a glass-fronted beehive and a chance to sample the finished product.

By 1925 horticulture was a well-established part of the show and gold medals were introduced for trade displays judged to be of special merit. Prior to this the prizes had been mere silver medals, with a silver cup for the overall winner. The new awards evidently went down well with competitors because, just two years later, three special Royal Crown Derby trophies were added to the spoils. And in 1928 it was announced that, in line with other societies in the area, the committee would award large gold and silver gilt medals to the best exhibits in the trade exhibition

Ruth Read (right) *with the flower judge and Betty Haller* (left) *admiring one of the entries at the 1984 show.*

Horticulture judges line up – Percy Thrower is third from the left. (McC)

Betty Haller (left) *and Ruth Read* (right) *watch Miss Hall putting the finishing touches to her flower arrangement.* (DT)

Admiring entries in the broad-bean competition.

The National Vegetable Society's magnificent display of vegetables in the horticulture tent.

Louise Baylis of Macclesfield entered this garden in the horticulture section. (CU)

Judging the entries in the floral-art tent.

section which, as today, involved awe-inspiring displays of the exhibitors' best produce – a chance for companies to show off their most popular lines and most abundant blooms.

The competitive classes at that time included an open section, another from which nurserymen and florists were barred, and a third confined specifically to cottagers and allotment holders within a ten-mile radius of Bakewell Church. This was the beginning of today's competitive classes for local amateur growers, keen gardeners and allotment holders, which attract entries from across the area.

By the time war broke out once again, the schedule had been extended to include a special competition for Women's Institutes – which now run a whole marquee in their own right. Honey classes had also become a regular feature, although these were not part of the main horticulture show across the area.

Horticulture prizes included the Royal Horticultural Society's Banksian Medal (bronze) for the winner of the most prize money in open classes, the Affiliated Societies Medal (silver gilt) for the exhibit judged most meritorious in open and local classes and the Sweet Pea Society's Silver Medal for the best sweet-pea exhibit. These endure to this day for presentation in competitive horticulture classes.

The non-competitive section for trade exhibitors was still a coveted event; the last pre-war show in 1939 attracted 20 trade exhibits from as far away as Sussex, Edinburgh, Norwich and Dorset. This continues to be the case, with the section perpetually over-subscribed and entry limited by invitation only – exhibitors are selected on merit, based on proven track records at regional and national shows. Many of them travel from all over Britain to take part and at least two exhibit only at Bakewell and the prestigious Chelsea Flower Show. Bakewell has a reputation for quality and its supporters are a loyal bunch. One family of nurserymen, Devine Nurseries from Humberside, have supported the show for up to three generations with stunning displays of cut flowers.

The 1950s brought growing recognition to Bakewell's horticultural show. The innovative bush tomato, developed by W.J. Unwins of Histon in Cambridge, made its debut at the 1952 event. The Amateur, as it was dubbed, was unlike any of its fore-runners, grown in beds like strawberries and never reaching more than a foot high.

In 1955 the show's stature was further boosted when several royal gardeners headed the team of judges. Mr C.H. Cook (of Windsor and Sandringham), Percy Thrower (formerly of Windsor Castle and by that time a well-known television expert) and Mr D. Stevenson (Windsor) all lent their expertise to the competitive classes. Percy Thrower must have enjoyed the experience – he was still making

Right: *Sweet peas on show in the horticultural tent at the 1984 show.* (SN)

Below: *Visitors are fascinated by the bees and the honey.* (DT)

Background image: *Derbyshire NFU's entry in the horticulture section.*

Below: *Jean Seat of Totley, vice-chairman of Sheffield Floral Art Club with her first prizewinning artwork which won the Ellen Mumby trophy.* (SN)

Left: *Wine entries in the wine section.*

Below left: *Valerie Hoole, chairman of Hope Valley Flower Club, with the winning entry in the Culinary Class for Small Clubs section.* (SN)

Below: *A competition was introduced for small well dressings – and the British and European Geranium Society responded, much to the delight of these visitors.*

BEST WINE OF THE SHOW

Blooming marvellous – part of the trade section in the horticulture marquee.

Small boys watching a flower arrangement taking shape.

VIP appearances at the show more than 20 years later.

Judges are always of national standing and Bakewell prides itself on the high quality of its entries. In those days a judge was appointed to each competition and everyone kept their fingers crossed that he or she would turn up at the appointed time. Things changed somewhat after an incident in the mid-'60s involving the associated floral-art competition. 'It was a scary moment,' recalls Betty Haller, a member of the horticulture committee for 40 years:

National judge Jean Taylor was coming from Cheshire to judge the floral art, but there was a car smash and when the prizes were due to be announced she hadn't turned up. We had a tent full of 100-plus exhibits and nobody to judge them!

Betty stepped into the breach and began the adjudication, until Jean arrived. 'But after that we decided that floral art should have more than one judge – and they should be on the premises before the day.'

There have actually been few changes to the show over the years. Pat Lunn, a professional horticulturalist and lecturer, has been involved with it since the 1970s and fills the role of chief steward of the trade section. She says the main differences are down to changing trends:

There are certain classes of display that sadly we no longer see but which used to provide us with a wealth of colour – like the dahlias and the roses. It's partly because they're difficult and expensive to display but also because they're out of fashion.

Trends in popular plants have changed the nature of the trade marquee. We now have a lot of alpines and rock plants, but the real 'in' thing is hardy herbaceous perenniels and they've really taken over.

Other more recent additions include wine classes, which were introduced around 20 years ago, and a special societies' competition for a display of fruit, flowers and vegetables.

Floral art has also taken an increasingly high profile in the show. Visitors – flower arrangers or otherwise – are fascinated by the stunning displays, the intricate arrangements and the inspired interpretation of themes. By 1991 this section had become so popular that the tent had to be extended and in 1999 it moved to become an integral part of the horticultural quarter.

The centenary of the horticultural section was celebrated in 1997: exactly 100 years since those first moves to amalgamate Bakewell's horticultural and agricultural societies. The occasion was marked by an extended complex and the launch of a new competition for scented carnations – two special classes were judged by show president William Mycock and have remained a regular feature ever since.

The centenary also saw the inauguration of the horticultural theatre, a stage area surrounded by seating, with a running programme of demonstrations by exhibitors. This too has become a fixture of the show, featuring practical demonstrations by nurserymen and florists and top tips from the experts on how to grow anything from exotic lillies to monster marrows.

Since 2000 it has also included a session called Ask the Gardening Experts – Bakewell's answer to Gardeners' Question Time. The inaugural event featured a panel headed by resident Radio Derby horticulturalist Anne Liverman, who bravely faced a barrage of questions posed by members of the audience.

But the success of the horticulture section lies not just with an action-packed programme of events, but also with the quality and quantity of entries... and that is down to the exhibitors, a dedicated and talented crew with inspiring commitment and interminable patience as well as green fingers.

Nurturing, growing and showing flowers, fruit and vegetables is an exact science and requires tremendous commitment. Tension reaches fever pitch along with excitement on the eve of show as staging is completed, potential prizewinning vegetables are lifted, perfect blooms are selected, and everything is carefully transported to the showground. 'There's a great camaraderie among the growers in the marquee but everyone tends to be a bit wound up to start with because they're all busy working on their exhibits,' said Pat Lunn:

Sometimes it takes them a couple of days, and more than one journey, to get everything to Bakewell. They work overnight on Tuesday to complete their displays and there's a general air of expectation as the time approaches for the results of the judging. The atmosphere is absolutely superb.

Things don't always go according to plan, of course. In 1978 one of the stalls mysteriously 'disappeared' during the night and officials had to rig up a hasty replacement the next morning. The following year nurseryman Andrew Derbyshire was putting the finishing touches to his stand when a runaway car came hurtling through the marquee, knocking him off his ladder. And then there's the weather. Pat Lunn recalls 2002 as being one of the wettest on record in the run-up to the show:

There was a deluge that just went on and on; the centre of the marquee was just a lake and virtually a no-go area for most of the show. Some wit brought a blow-up crocodile to stand guard over it – and a sign that said 'no swimming'!

Another year, following the death of a committee member, the horticulture chairman promised to arrange the staging of floral-art displays. But when the committee turned up to prepare for the show, they found nothing had been done. Betty Haller recalls:

A tractor brought over a load of staging, but by 11am no-one had appeared to put it up. Eventually a chap came into the tent carrying a small carpenter's bag – the tent was about 140ft x 60ft and they'd sent just one man!

She put in an emergency call to her husband and he arrived with a team of friends to help out: 'They worked all day and half the night. The next day my husband couldn't walk round the show because he was absolutely jiggered!' At the end of the show committee member Jack Goudy – who trained in horticulture at Kew – volunteered to supervise the dismantling. He called in a group of British Legion members, including Alan Dunn, and instructed them in how to construct the staging. Alan and his team have been in charge of floral-art staging ever since and these days their wives are roped in too, to paint all the backgrounds. The results are so good that they are setting the standard for other shows across the country. Betty came across a member of Gateshead Show photographing and measuring the designs so she could copy them for her own event.

This compliment is indicative of the show's standing. These days competitive entries run into hundreds, in a total of more than 150 classes: 109 in the purely horticultural sections plus another 32 for honey and 12 for wine. There are usually in the region of 1,000 exhibits in the competitive classes and up to three dozen stands in the trade section. So big is the show that it occupies the largest marquees on the ground: 300ft x 90ft for the trade section, plus a 140ft x 40ft annexe for competitive classes and yet another for the floral art.

The show's impressive reputation has helped to attract a number of horticultural societies which, in recent years, have held their own national and provincial shows in conjunction with Bakewell. These include the National Sweet Pea Society, the British National Carnation Society and the Royal National Rose Society. Bakewell is also affiliated to the Royal Horticultural Society, the National Vegetable Society and the National Beekeepers' Association, which all award special prizes at the show.

The Duchess of Rutland presents a trophy to the winner of one the horse classes, the year her husband was president of the show.

High Peak and Barlow Hunts celebrating hunting through the ages in a special centre-ring parade.

Twenty-Two

Horses

One of the most difficult decisions faced by organisers of the foot-and-mouth-hit show in 2001 was whether or not to ban horses as well as livestock from the showground. For they knew that from Shires to Shetlands show-goers had a huge affection for the horse classes and not allowing them to come to Bakewell would leave an unbridgable gap. Horses themselves were not at risk, but many were stabled in or around farmland and in the end the possibility of spreading the disease was just too great. So there was no showjumping, no heavy-horse turnouts, no Hackneys, no mounted games – in fact the list of horse-related attractions which were absent that year is so long, one might wonder how the show carried on at all. This just serves to underline the important relationship which Bakewell Show enjoys with the equine world. But it has always been so, even from the earliest days. The working and harness horses may not have had the profile of a farm's prize bull, but they were still a vital part of the agricultural team, and were recognised as such. Indeed the breeding of good utility heavy horses for working on the land or for transport was actively encouraged with classes and special prizes.

In the last part of the nineteenth century the schedule was extended to include hunters and riding horses and at the 1892 show the Duke of Devonshire, a keen breeder of Shire horses, sponsored the classes for 'the best plough horse, draught kind and best fitted for breeding hunters.'

This was a golden period for the Shire horse which carried on into the first decade of the next century. With growing demand from abroad for English hunters, the hunter breed classes were increased and other classes were introduced over the following years as different breeds grew in popularity.

In the early part of the twentieth century they would arrive at the showground on hoof if they were close enough or by train if they lived further afield, with their grooms in attendance on the journey. But as Bakewell's reputation grew, competitors would come from all over the country using another kind of horsepower – with the owners at the wheels of their own horseboxes and trailers.

The horse section is one which has always been there, quietly and efficiently pleasing both visitors and competitors with little fuss and seemingly even less publicity. It has only been in recent years, with the

Joshua Tetley & Son brewery dray on parade at the show. (CU)

Above: *Beautifully dressed in traditional attire – a Shire horse on parade at the 2002 show.*

Left: *Nine-year-old Ashley Beighton of Ashover with pony Tavistock Jamboree which was awarded the John Smallman trophy for the best local pony in the show in 1978.* (DT)

Right: *The High Peak Hounds – a popular centre-ring attraction.*

Bottom: *Entrants line up in the children's pony class.* (McC)

advent of the country's top showjumpers at the show and the introduction of exciting new breeds reflecting the changing interest by horse owners, that its profile has been raised to its rightful place. Fourteen-year-old David Morrison may not have been a top name at the 1977 show, but he certainly hit the headlines with his victory in the junior showjumping. Riding Calton Lees Rockafella, he beat a tough field of 30 to take the Kerrygold Junior Foxhunter title. What made his victory more admirable was the fact that the nine-year-old chestnut mare was lucky to be at the show at all. She had badly cut one hind leg on a barbed-wire fence earlier in the year and sprained the other when she broke loose at her owner's Wingerworth farm and tried to leap a passing car.

It was international showjumper Harvey Smith's boys, Robert and Stephen, who were lucky to be at the show the following year. Harvey – no stranger to publicity himself – had approached the show director John Smallman at the Royal International Horse Show and asked if they could compete in the National Westminster Stakes which carried an £80 first prize. Unfortunately, because entries had already closed, they were turned down. Then British team manager Ronnie Massarella said he needed Caroline Bradley, Graham Fletcher and Malcolm Pyrah to ride for Britain at Hickstead on 3 August which clashed with Bakewell where they were all due to appear. Their absence enabled the show to do a U-turn and invite the Smith brothers. As John Smallman said at the time:

Caroline Bradley, Graham Fletcher and Malcolm Pyrah appearing at Hickstead depleted our showjumping entries and we didn't want to deprive the public of the star jumpers.

Harvey Smith was later to suggest that the organisers might delay closing entries until two weeks before the show to give principal riders an idea of the condition and availability of themselves and their horses. The request was considered, but not granted because leaving entries so late would have seriously delayed publication of the whole livestock catalogue. Other top names were able to appear, however, including Nick Skelton, Liz Edgar and Michael and John Whitaker, together with Michael Saywell, fresh from his triumph at the Royal International where, riding Trevor Banks' horse Chair Bridge, he had won the *Daily Mail* Cup.

Bakewell was still not officially a two-day show, although on what was termed the 'preview' day showjumpers competed for the Kerrygold Junior Foxhunter, Machon Bank Motor Junior Jumping and the E.T. Sutherland Junior Open Jumping championships.

On show day proper the Derbyshire Area International Showjumping trial – a qualifier for the Horse of the Year Show in October – took place along

with competitions for Shire horses, working-hunter ponies, children's show ponies, riding pony breeding classes, novice ponies, Shetland ponies, Welsh Mountain and mixed Mountain and Moorland ponies.

Rumours abounded at the 1979 show that Captain Mark Philips, then the Queen's son-in-law, might put in an appearance. Olympic winner Hideaway was scheduled to take part in a showjumping event and Captain Philips was the last person to ride him – as it turned out he did not come. Neither, according to newspaper reports, did any Arab horses. The classes had to be cancelled because they clashed with the National Arab Show being staged at Ascot. But the breed was back with a vengeance the following year – making a triumphant return with a creditable 60 entries. That year saw a record 750 horses and ponies entered in the various classes – excluding the five showjumping events. A new class for plucky little Haflingers attracted 11 entries and children's show ponies 142. The winner of the Derbyshire Area International Trial that year collected £265 in winnings. One horse which was applauded for its courage in 1979 wasn't strictly part of the horse section. Royal Canadian mounted policeman Joe Roberts riding Lady Athene put on a spectacular display of horsemanship in the centre ring. It included gymnastics on horseback and a dangerous feat of riding through six flaming straw bales complete with thunder flashes.

The year 1981 saw Caroline Bradley, Liz and Ted Edgar, and Yorkshire's rising star Mark Fuller making an appearance. Popular rider Paddy McMahon entered too, on Tigre. But it was Derbyshire teenager Sarah Betteridge who stole the limelight. Sarah from Brailsford had already qualified for the Horse of the Year Show on her mounts Forever Diamonds and Onedin II, and had just returned from Brussels, where the previous week she had won the individual Grand Prix, riding for Britain. She compounded her Belgian success by being placed in the E.T. Sutherland Open, the Saab Open and the *Daily Mail*/Christy Beaufort Junior Showjumper qualifier. The following year saw the appearance of Richard Arthers, a 15-year-old from Newton Solney, a member of the Meynell Pony Club team which had qualified for Hickstead. As a qualifier

Showjumper in action. (DT)

for the Horse of the Year Show, Bakewell continued to attract all the top names and in 1986 the flamboyant Harvey Smith made his debut heading one of the most impressive line-ups since 1971.

The 1980s and '90s were to set the seal on the horse section which, because of its variety, has wide appeal to show-goers. The Hackneys have always had a special place in the hearts of show folk. Few in number – mainly because of the high cost of maintenance – they are tremendously stylish and greatly admired. Originally known as the Norfolk trotter, they were general-purpose horses, used in the nineteenth century for ploughing and taking the farmer's wife to market. Later they would take part in trotting races until eventually they developed into the Hackney – from the French 'haquenee', meaning 'riding horse' – which became famed and loved for its extravagant gait.

Another much-loved horse is the Shire and the heavy-horse classes at the show are tremendously popular. In the 1990s Britain had a strong export market in heavy horses, particularly to America, and at Bakewell visitors saw the best. Mainly bays, some were working horses and others were kept specially for showing. Up until the 1950s and '60s, heavy horses were the mainstay of rural life, working the land and transporting goods. Today there are few working horses, most being kept on farms as pets or by diehard breeders and breweries for shows and festivals. Preparing a Shire horse for the show begins at the start of the year as Steve Flewitt, show judge and stalwart of the horse section, testifies:

It takes a lot of dedication to get heavy horses into the peak of show condition. It's not just a case of visiting the stable every two or three hours and chucking a bucket of feed at them – it's a lot of hard work.

Curiously for such powerful animals, they do not require a lot of protein, but they do need around 50lbs a day of hay, sugarbeet and molasses. In the winter their hair is allowed to grow long and thick and the silky hair around their feet must be oiled several times a month to keep out the dirt and stop any infection. They are shampooed two or three times week and dried under a solarium. When the summer comes the horses are re-shod with heavy steel bevel shoes ready for their appearance. Keeping them clean can be something of a nightmare, given that the majority of Shires live in farm fields, but the day before the show they are washed and dried again. On show day their legs get an extra wash and brush-up and baby powder

or french chalk is massaged in to give them that an extra lift. Plaiting the mane is an art in itself, then the brasses and leathers need to be burnished, but the spectacle they make is worth every minute of the effort. Shires may be spectacular, but hunters are magnificent – and judging entries in this class must seem interminable. Because it is a qualifier for the Horse of the Year Show, competitors come from all over the country, eagerly hoping to make the grade. Judging begins at 8a.m. on the Wednesday and judges do not simply examine the horses, but ride each one and give marks for a comfortable ride.

The mounted games is a popular attraction and one of the highlights of the centre-ring programme. The competition features teams of young riders testing their skills of horsemanship, agility and speed and involves vaulting, bending and turning at a breathtaking pace. Traditionally it is an inter-county event, but in 1992 it involved young riders from Sweden, Scotland and Wales.

Another centre-ring spectacle is the ladies' sidesaddle event. No longer the only way for a respectable woman to ride a horse, this class recognises the ability to ride in this style while looking graceful, composed, balanced and dignified. With horses 'back in the saddle' at the 2002 show, numbers are continuing to rise along with Bakewell's reputation as one of the top 25 horse shows in the country, a standing underlined by Robin Rhodes, president for 2002:

I met a competitor who had gone to the show office to collect his certificate for sixth place. He told me that sixth place at Bakewell was the equivalent of a first at many other shows.

A fine Shire horse and cart at the show.

Dogs arriving for the 1974 show. (DT)

Judging the dog show championship.

Twenty-Three

The Dog Section

They have been man's best friend for centuries, but dogs have also been a friend to Bakewell Show over the years – even if it did take almost six decades before they were officially introduced into the proceedings. Their debut at the 1878 show was, by today's standards, a low-key affair with just 130 entries, including 26 shepherd dogs and 33 fox terriers – but Lord George Cavendish MP joined in the spirit of the occasion and brought along five gun dogs, two retrievers and three setters for visitors to see, although he sportingly didn't enter into the competition.

The new classes seem to have caught the public imagination because dogs, along with pigeons and poultry, were picked out for particular mention in show records for the mid-1880s. On one occasion a creditable 213 dogs turned up... along with nine cats, which were entered in the 'best cat – any variety' class in 1892. Quite what happened between then and 1905 is not certain, but that year, for some strange reason, the dogs, together with the poultry, were abandoned, only to be reintroduced, according to historian Lance Waud, in 1908.

After the First World War, however, dogs seem to have gained momentum again and the section grew both in terms of the numbers of dogs being entered and the different breeds. In complete contrast to the two or three different breeds on offer when the dogs were first seen at Bakewell, the 1924 show included classes for Sealyhams, Retrievers, Collies, Airedales, Pomeranians, Spanish Bulldogs, Pekingese and Alsatian Wolfdogs.

In the 1930s the dog section was sponsored by Spillers Osoko dog food. The name not only appeared on every page of the catalogue, but the company also urged all the exhibitors to support the committee's policy of using Spillers' foods, with the catalogue declaring: 'All dogs will be fed on Osoko the

paramount dog food and puppies on Saval, the practical puppy rearing food.' Whether this caused some comment is not documented, but in a message to exhibitors the show secretary acknowledged:

Whilst they acquire certain advertising privileges in return, we are assured that Spillers' primary object in benching and feeding dog shows is to encourage the breeding and exhibiting of pedigree dogs.

Charles Fairs took over the chairmanship of the dog section in the 1940s and over the next 20 years built it into a large and important component of the show. It was during his tenure that a Kennel Club ruling had a serious effect on entries. The club announced a national ban on litter classes which came into force before the show in 1962. As a result entries dropped by more than 100 on the previous year's record. The ban was a particular blow to visitors for whom the litter benches had been one of the biggest attractions at the dog show in the past – and for exhibitors who had always seen Bakewell as a first-class shop-window for their puppies.

Charles Fairs worked tirelessly for the section and when he and his wife celebrated their golden wedding anniversary, the general committee marked the milestone with an inscribed silver salver. Sadly Mr Fairs died a couple of years later, and his deputy Frank Twiggs took over as chairman.

Throughout the 1970s the dog section continued to attract a huge following. In 1976 organisers had to call a halt when entries reached a staggering 2,250. Two years later 2,200 entries were recorded at the 1978 show – and an up-and-coming breed hit the headlines. There were only 50 bouvier des Flandres dogs in Britain – and two of them made an appearance at Bakewell. Nelson and Kookie belonged to the

Above: *Final preparation for the judges.*

Right: *Keeping their feet dry – two Old English sheepdogs arrive at the show.* (DT)

Opposite page: *English bull terrier Meg and Staffordshire bull terrier Beth at the 1992 show.* (DET)

Dog show championship.

Lucas family who ran a dog-breeding business in Creswell, Derbyshire. Originally mongrel cattle dogs in Belgium, they had become a well-known breed on the Continent where they were used by several police forces. Kookie crowned her appearance by coming first in the novice rare-breeds class.

By the end of the decade the number of entries was becoming a logistical nightmare, as Frank Twiggs recalled:

Exhibitors travelled from all parts of the country and some have been so delayed by traffic that they failed to arrive in time for their classes. We could not have waited because it was essential that dog show judging began on time at 10am in order to get through the large entry.

I remember many years ago we had to bring the cars around the ringside and switch on the headlights in order to complete the judging. That was 10 o'clock at night.

Eventually in 1980 – by which time Dorrie Patterson had taken over as chairman – the whole dog section was moved to the preview show day and this opened the door to Bakewell becoming a two-day show the following year.

A curious thing happened at the first two-day show, although there is nothing to suggest a connection. The Dewar White Label Perpetual Challenge Cup for the best exhibit in the show suddenly reappeared after going missing for a couple of years. The winner of the trophy in 1978 had failed to return it so it had not been awarded during the previous two shows. Nobody was spotted bringing it back; it mysteriously appeared on the secretary's table – which was good news for a Dachshund owned by Bill Pinches of Bilston in the West Midlands who took it home.

A two-day show meant more time to fill and secretary Ted Brownhill decided that one of the attractions should be a demonstration on the Wednesday by Wirksworth Dog Obedience Club. The club had been set up in 1978 and until then had demonstrated only at various well-dressing celebrations and other outdoor summer events. This was to be their biggest booking yet and Ted declared: 'The club will come along and give demonstrations for beginners right through to advanced.'

There were other dogs on the showground too in the shape of the High Peak Harrier Hounds, which had a proud history dating back more than 150 years. They gave demonstrations in the centre ring for a number of years. And the inter-county sheepdog trials were held at the show too.

By the 1990s Bakewell had consolidated its position as one of the biggest and most prestigious open dog shows in the North of England. And the dog interest at the show now had a permanent spot on the Thursday too. It started in 1993 with displays of dog agility and obedience and continued with something of a coup the following year. Sheila Bailey, a member of the UK Registry of Canine Behaviour, and full-time canine consultant with Derbyshire Canine Centre, organised a series of demonstrations designed to show dog owners how to live happily with their pets.

Four years later the honours went to John Whiteley who entertained the centre-ring crowds with his sheepdog and farmyard display. And the doyenne of dog training, Katie Patmore, also gave a demonstration based on the Kennel Club's Good Citizens dog scheme when visitors with family pets were invited into the ring to learn some tricks and take part in a dog obedience session.

The building of the Agricultural Business Centre and the subsequent reorganisation of the showground meant a new home for the dog section and now, having overcome a few teething problems, it seems to have settled down. The open dog show is held on both show days with more than 120 different breeds represented including the lesser-known varieties of Ibizan hound, Basset Fauve de Bretagne, Havanese, Lowechen (little lion dog), Leonburger and a Segugio Italiano.

In 2001, when livestock was not allowed because of the foot-and-mouth crisis, the dog section really flew the flag for Bakewell Show and in line with the 'family show' emphasis that year introduced junior handling classes for the first time. There were four classes specifically for the under-17s with the winners qualifying for the Junior Handler of the Year at the Richmond Championship Show at Ascot.

The high profile clearly paid off because in 2002, amid falling entries for other open dog shows, Bakewell had another record-breaking entry. Dorrie Patterson was delighted:

It's phenomenal in this climate – the last 18 months has seen a real decline in entries at open dog shows. It started with the foot and mouth and then breeders started looking at how much it cost to enter and saw not entering as a way of saving money.

But over the last five years we have built up a reputation for putting on a good show and we have some of the best facilities anyone could expect. The entrance is convenient, the judges well-respected and we put on new breeds every year.

But as much as anything it is down to the hard work of the committee, who don't just send out entry forms, they go out of their way to talk to people as well.

Left to right, above: *A Pekingese dog all fluffed up and ready to show*; *Doug Skelton prepares his dog Allicia for the judges* (SN); *High Peak Hounds taking part in the centre-ring display.*

Right: *Under inspection by the dog show judge.*

Below: *Admiring glances for one dog show entrant.*

Getting ready for the dog show judging.

Twenty-Four

Men and Machines

In the early days it was largely sheer sweat and toil which kept the farms going... unless, of course, you were a wealthy landowner and could afford to experiment with the new inventions constantly being unveiled. But one of the reasons why the society was founded in the first place was to keep small farmers up to date with developments, and that meant machinery as well as husbandry.

Although the first shows were largely a celebration of livestock and to a certain extent crops, by the 1830s agricultural machinery had begun to stir up interest. John Spencer is reported to have sold several of the machines he invented for chopping hay and straw at the 1832 show. And two years later Robert Arkwright brought along a one-horse tipping cart he had designed which, despite (as previously mentioned) weighing nine cwts and having 4$\frac{1}{2}$in iron tyres, was actually said to be more manoeuvrable.

A new clod crusher made its debut in the early 1840s, the brainchild of a Mr Crosskill, who managed to export a large number to Russia. But a Mr Nicholson took the honours at the 1848 show with his improved cake-breaking machine, which sliced through cotton cake with an ease that amazed all the onlookers.

By the turn of the century, there were machines for doing any number of agricultural tasks – as advertised in the 1923 show catalogue by Wm Britt of South Street, Chesterfield. There were Bamford's mill, chaff cutters and pulpers, Hornsby's brinders, ploughs and drills, Blackstone's swathe turner and horse rakes, Diabolo separators and Lister's butter churns. Also that year W. Hand, authorised Ford dealer of Matlock, offered a Fordson Tractor with three-and-a-half-ton trailer for £315 complete.

The balance switched in the twentieth century from the inventors demonstrating and selling their machines direct to the farmers, to agricultural machinery dealers using Bakewell Show as a shop-window for their products. The show was a rare day out for the farmer who would take full advantage, not just to see the latest tractor or driller, but to enjoy the good old-fashioned hospitality on offer.

But in the latter part of the century, as the economy changed so did the farmers' way of buying new machinery. The golden days of British agriculture were waning and with them opportunities to sell new tractors to farmers. Dealers found it increasingly difficult to justify the cost of exhibiting at the show so they had no choice but to stop coming.

Fortunately by the end of the 1990s things had improved enough for them to re-assert themselves. But there is still a tremendous affection for the 'old stuff' and the vintage farm machinery is a very popular area with visitors, particularly older show-goers who can actually remember using some of it as youngsters.

Stalwart of the show's vintage vehicle section, Terry Robinson, can understand their feelings – he got hooked as a 13-year-old when, together with farmer John Burnett of Wye Farm, Rowsley, he restored a 1957 grey-and-gold Fergie. It had been standing in the shed for a number of years and been all but dismantled. They managed to salvage some of the missing parts from the dump and beg, borrow and buy the rest from local farmyard sales. The biggest expenditure was the gold paint for the engine which cost £18 a litre. Terry went on to restore other machines – his favourite was a rare Morris Bamlett mower, one of only three such machines made at Wye Farm in the early 1930s.

As so often in agriculture it was a case of 'needs must'. In those days teams of Irish labourers would come to the farm during the haymaking and do the work in return for a meal and a drink. But when hard times hit the farm, even that bill was too expensive, so John Burnett decided to develop a machine to do the work. He married the transmission from a Morris Cowley with a Bamlett mower and produced the machine which was such a success that people came from all over the area to get a look at it. It was so popular that it had be locked away each night so that it didn't get accidentally damaged by the men it had put out of work. The Morris Bamlett was the first machine to be used to mow Chatsworth Park, and spent many years in the Chatsworth museum before being removed in the mid-1980s. By then it was in a sorry state; not only had the engine seized up, but it needed a new clutch, petrol tank and bonnet, which had rotted away.

Terry couldn't find a radiator to match so the original one had to be repaired. It took months of dedication from Terry and two fellow enthusiasts, Philip Heathcote and Nigel Wilde, but eventually the mower was restored to its former glory and went on show again. The machine proved a star turn at local shows, failing only once, ironically at Bakewell Show, when it refused to start. Terry recalls:

The magneto had stood for too long and there was damp inside. We didn't have much choice but to tow her back to the farm from the showground on the Wednesday night and work on her. Fortunately there was an old bloke who used to have a bit of a fairground on the farm and he gave us the bit we needed to get her going again.

They worked all night and by eight o'clock the next morning they were back on the showground.

Over the years one of the oldest machines exhibited at Bakewell has been a stationary engine dating back to 1901, brought by David Hall of Longnor. It, like all the other old machines on display at the show, has a certain fascination for visitors. Nostalgia plays a big part, harking back to the heady days of haymaking in the last century, but it's also a tribute to these plucky little machines which, with all the sophisticated advances in agricultural machinery, can still hold their own and be useful around the farm if they are needed.

Left: *Vintage tractors are a popular feature of the show, pictured here in 2002.*

Below: *Letting off steam – engines at the show.* (SN)

❧ Twenty-Five ❧

The Secret of Success

Unquestionably, one has to be dedicated to compete at Bakewell Show. It doesn't matter if you are a showjumper or stockman, rabbit breeder or vegetable veteran, it's the months of hard work put in beforehand which really matter; the two show days – fun as they are – are merely the icing on top of the metaphorical cake. Not that many of the 50,000 visitors who gaze longingly at the leeks and admiringly at the Ayrshires actually realise this, but fellow competitors do, and that's what counts.

For showjumpers it is months of practice and perfect timing which will help score points and win trophies, but for growers and stock breeders it is a combination of know-how and hands-on work throughout the year.

As far as horticulture is concerned, Bakewell comes early in the show calendar – too early for the real monster onions and other veg. But that doesn't stop it being a Mecca for competitors from as far away as the North West and Scotland. There tend to be fewer entries from the south – local growers like to think that is because they don't like to lose to their northern brothers, because they, like all the other green-fingered experts, know that you have to be good to win at Bakewell, and that is their aim.

So what is the secret? Stan Dickinson – stalwart of the Horticulture Committee and its chairman for several years in the 1990s, as well as an exhibitor for more than four decades – knows only too well. The answer, to coin that well-known horticultural phrase... lies in the soil. Perfectly balanced soil will produce prize-winning vegetables; but soil which is out of sorts will only produce crops fit for the pot. So how do they get the balance right? They need to talk to the experts, and that means gathering samples of the soil from the vegetable patch and sending it, together with details of the crops they wish to grow, to a soil specialist to have it analysed. The soil specialist will then write back with details of exactly what steps the grower should take to achieve perfection. The report is detailed and includes the pH of the soil, the lime treatment required, the level of nitrogen, phosphate and potassium, a fertiliser formula and a feeding programme tailored to the kind of vegetables to be grown. Now, with the 'formula for success' in his hands, the grower can begin the long journey to the show bench.

Seeds for prize-winning onions are sown in December in a warm greenhouse. When they reach the 'crook' stage, where they are bending over slightly, they are transferred to three-inch pots, followed by five-inch pots and finally polytunnels or cold-frames outside. The ground where the onions will reach fruition is prepared in accordance with the soil report and farmyard manure is added for good measure. Then, in April, the seedlings are planted out. At this point they are sprayed to protect them from onion fly and other pests and diseases which might kill them.

Over the next few weeks the onions are fed with high-nitrogen food which promotes root growth, but once they have started to 'bulb' in the third week in June they are fed with potash to help them ripen. Three weeks before the show is when the intensive work begins. The onions are gently lifted with a fork, the roots washed and the tops cut off. All the loose scales are stripped away and the onions are washed, dried and dusted with baby powder before being wrapped in kitchen towels and stored on a special tray. After that the grower can do nothing more except keep his fingers crossed. If it's an eight pounder he stands a good chance of a rosette – few people manage to field much heavier than that because the show is held so early.

Show-stopping leeks require quite different handling – the secret with them is to choose seedlings from Wales, which grow much bigger than the regular kitchen variety. Once all the soil analyst's instructions have been followed and the leek has started to develop, it needs blanching for showing. This is achieved by wrapping black cloth around the vegetable and leaving it in place until it is ready to show. Prize-winning leeks are a joy to behold, straight and proud like sentries guarding a winning arrangement.

For cauliflowers, success lies in the curd – and perfect timing. If it has started to separate, even only slightly, it can't be shown. And the secret of rich curd? Plenty of manure and gallons of water, according to Stan. Once again the seeds are planted early – Elby is one of the most popular varieties at Bakewell – and only transferred outside when the plants are deemed hardy enough. The leaves continue to grow and when they have reached around two feet, the grower will look for the curd. Once it has been located he will tie

Time for a break – stockman with hungry cow.

Champion Ayrshire cow. (McC)

The Old Original Bakewell Pudding Shop is a regular exhibitor in the British food and farming marquee.

After months of nurturing the prize vegetables go on show.

Left: *Making friends – girl and goat.*

Below left: *Putting the finishing touches to a floral display.*

Below: *Dry-stone-walling demonstration at the 1984 show.* (DT)

Above: *Perfect eggs.*

Left: *Roland Boocock, show secretary for seven years.*

Above: *From wax jackets and walking sticks to oriental treasures... trade stands are great money earners for the show.*

Above right: *Jed Hone's Strolling Jazz Band – always a popular attraction at the show.*

Right: *A craftsman at work.*

Left: *St Bernards with bibs at the ready so that they don't spoil their freshly-groomed coats*

Above: *Visitors walk from the new Bakewell Agricultural Business Centre.*

Left: *The Show Office on show day with the flower-beds all full.*

Clockwise from above:
*A couple of Shetland
ponies arrive for the
show in 1974* (DT);
*Making friends with
one of the entrants in the
poultry section, 1974* (DT);
*David Dillon from main
show sponsors, the Gordon
Lamb Group, presenting a
commemorative horse brass
to one lucky winner;
Cheese winner – with
wine of course;
A proud cup
winner*
(McC).

up the leaves to keep out the daylight and wait... In ten days it should be perfect for the show bench.

At least the cauliflower grower knows what he can expect before the show. The poor grower of carrots on the other hand has to wait until the eve of the event before he knows if he even has something worth showing. Unlike onions, leeks or cauliflowers, carrots are grown in 45-gallon drums filled with sand. Holes are bored into the sand with a broom handle and filled with peat, into which clusters of seeds are planted. Stan takes up the story:

Each cluster is covered with a jam jar with the bottom knocked out which acts like a kind of cloche and they are left until they germinate. The strongest seedlings are then selected from each cluster and the weakest are pulled out leaving just five individual plants.

From then on in it's down to luck. All you can do is to spray them to keep them free from carrot fly and keep the 'shoulders' covered so they don't go green and trust that the carrot finds its way straight to the bottom of the drum without bending or forking.

Unfortunately it is impossible to tell, until the night before, exactly what is in the barrel, and then it's crunch time.

When you are ready for lifting you tip gallons of water in to flood the drum and gradually keep working the carrot loose so that hopefully you won't break the stem.

When you hear a loud sucking noise it should come free and, with luck, you have a long, straight three- or four-foot carrot.

It's not documented how many carrots fail to make the grade, by forking, bending or breaking at the last minute, because horticulturalists manage to cover their disappointment well, but even those without green fingers can imagine the frustration.

There can be frustration too for competitors showing livestock and other animals; they also have a lot of nurturing to do if they want to stand a chance of being among the prizewinners.

For stockmen the frustration often lies in the inability of potential prizewinning beasts to stay clean! But their journey to the champion's rosette starts much earlier – from when the calves are born. A good stockman will spot a quality calf at birth, but that's not to say it will turn into a champion. The key is in the growth rate and it is usually at around three months that a farmer can see whether or not he has a potential winner on his hands.

Training for the show ring starts early; even if a calf is still being suckled it is regularly singled out from the rest of the herd, haltered and led around the yard to get it used to being handled. Some calves take to it straight away, others need longer before they are used to the attention, which also includes a regular wash

down, so shampooing for the show doesn't come as too much of a surprise.

Diet is important too to keep the beasts in tip-top condition and often comprises a mix of cereals, beef nuts and minerals. As the show approaches they are fed on dairy cake, hay and sugar-beet pulp.

Grooming for the show begins on the farm. Would-be prizewinning cattle are put in small stalls to restrict their movement and rubbed and scrubbed with soapy water before being towelled or rubbed dry with sawdust. A good buff down with a dandy brush follows and then each hoof is carefully clipped before the animals are turned into a clean straw-lined barn to wait for the truck to take them to the show.

But don't imagine for one minute that they stay in this pristine condition until after the judging. Cattle are messy creatures and stockmen must keep a constant vigil to spot cow pats before they can do any harm. That, and mopping up cows which have made a mess of themselves, can keep them very busy. And chances are they will still need washing at least once more before they go in the show ring. But it's more than worth it according to the farmers. They may invest a lot of sweat and hard work, but success on the show circuit can reap rich rewards and increase the value of a herd significantly.

Another vital ingredient is showmanship. Even with a potential champion beast a farmer who doesn't know how to show it to its best advantage can fail, whereas a farmer with a wealth of experience can make even an average cow into a champion. It is the same for sheep – the pathway to success lies in the preparation, and preparing a long-woolled Suffolk sheep for showing needs all the talent of a top stylist. But it's worth it in the end. For many farmers Bakewell Show is a massive advertising campaign which definitely pays dividends; top winners at the show can sell for several thousands of pounds.

Sheep chosen for showing are firstly given a good wash before being treated with a bloom dip, which acts as a sort of conditioner. Their fleece is then styled into a good square shape by carding the wool with a special comb to fluff it up and then it is trimmed again. Almost as much attention is paid to the animal's face which is cleaned and then smeared with baby oil to make it soft. Finally it is wrapped in a special coat to keep it clean until judging.

Short-woolled breeds such as Texels, on the other hand, require much less fuss. Judges don't want them to be 'dressed' so stockmen just wash their faces and legs in warm soapy water and give them a rub with a towel.

There are no such shortcuts for the poultry fraternity though. Any show-goer who thought that all that was required of a poultry exhibitor was a trawl around the yard to procure the plumpest bird, should talk to poultry supremo Frank Clarke. Frank, who is chairman of the Pigeons and Poultry Committee and who will be president in 2005, has spent many long hours in what could pass as a mini beauty salon preparing birds for the show.

The birds are taken to a special bathing area where they languish in washing-up-liquid bubbles to make sure they are clean. Their feathers are blown dry and fluffed up. Frank then gives each bird a 'manicure' cleaning out all the awkward little crevices with a cocktail stick. There is, he says, no substitute for preparation: 'You must get every leg scale clean, it is sometimes the difference between winning and coming second if there are two birds of equal quality.'

The work starts a good week before the show to allow time for the birds to replenish their natural oils. They are then kept in special pens lined with white wood shavings until show time when they can crow about their condition…

Preparing rabbits for showing takes much less time – indeed too much pampering is a disqualifiable offence. The key to success lies not in the work on the day, or indeed in the run up to the show, but on the holistic approach. Rabbits must be kept clean and healthy all the time and out of the draught and the damp – give them those conditions and they will look after themselves.

Spotting a champ in a newborn litter is something of a lottery. Experts can sometimes tell if one is a potential winner, but they can't tell for sure until the rabbit is about four months old when it has been through a moult. By then it will have become quite used to being handled and being groomed, two or three times a week to help through the moult of three separate coats. Here experience is paramount as too much grooming can spoil a good show rabbit.

So back to show day and, unlike the cattle, sheep and poultry, there is no beauty routine to be endured – all rabbits need is a gentle brush and rub-down with a moist cloth followed by a little polishing with a piece of velvet or silk and they're ready to shine.

Bakewell Show takes some licking!

Looking after the treasured show trophies.

Fancy That!

In 1844, at the society's dinner, the landlord of the Rutland Arms, William Greaves, who was also a farmer, was extolling the virtues of growing a herb called comfrey. The three-times-a-year crop was hardy and could be fed to cows without affecting the taste of their milk. Nearly 160 years later a huge industry has grown around the herb which is not only used for culinary and medicinal purposes, but also makes a good organic manure for feeding plants.

☞ At the 1848 show a special prize – three guineas given by Mr J.J. Rowley of Palterton – was awarded to 'the tenant farmer within the district of the society who shall have his farm house and building spouted in the most efficient manner so as to prevent rain water mixing with the farm yard manure' – the value of liquid manure was appreciated even then.

☞ One outstanding feature of the 1848 show was the huge black stallion of great power and substance brought from Flanders by George Stephenson earlier that year. It is thought to have been a specimen breed which played a part in breeding the Scarsdale Blacks and in shaping the conformation of the Shire horse, then in the course of being developed as a specific breed.

☞ A unique trade stand put in an appearance at the show in the last year of the nineteenth century. Whether the Mutual Life Assurance Company of New York, which specialised in all aspects of agricultural insurance, actually did any business is not recorded.

☞ In 1989 the 137th show was followed, not by the 138th, but by the 159th. Lance Waud discovered a mix-up which had robbed the society of 22 years of its rightful history. It happened when, in 1949, efforts were made to discover when the centenary should be celebrated. Various dates were thrown up including the founding of Bakewell Farmers' Club in 1843, the first show in 1849 and the reconciliation with North Derbyshire Agricultural Society in 1853. Since they couldn't agree they decided to brand the 1951 show the centenary event to coincide with the Festival of Britain. Hence they went from the 91st annual show in 1950 to the 100th in 1951. The fact is though that the unbroken link can be traced back to 1819, and even taking away the 12 years when the show was not held (because of foot and mouth in 1883 and the two world wars) Bakewell Show is still one of the oldest such events in the country.

☞ Showground co-ordinator Mike Patterson remembers a trade stand called The Wally Shop which sold furry bees in various poses. When the stallholder complained bitterly because she wasn't located on the main avenue he explained it was for upmarket goods only. She departed in high dudgeon. The following year she reappeared with... The Welly Shop, selling high-class hunter wellies, on the main avenue. She had transformed her business and got the spot she wanted.

A stockman getting a beast ready to be shown, watched by mums and children.

A crowd of show-goers waiting for the centre-ring entertainment.

Subscribers

Brian F. Bakel, Beeley, Matlock, Derbyshire

Isobel C. Bennett, Baslow, Derbyshire

Peter A. Bennett, Baslow, Derbyshire

Mr E. Boam, Ashleigh, Flagg

Mr T.W. Brocklehurst, Ashford, Bakewell

Richard G. Brown, Buxton, Derbyshire

Bob Burgin and Christine Windle, Sheffield

Edward J. Caudwell, Snitterton, Matlock, Derbyshire

Sandy Caudwell, Rowsley, Derbyshire

Major General Peter Cavendish, Middleton, Bakewell

Mr Kenneth Chadbourne, Moira

Mr Frank Clark, Ambergate, Derbyshire

Mary Daybell, Badger's Clough, Buxton

Andrew Derbyshire, Bakewell, Derbyshire

Stephen Flint, Kirkash Stud, Kirkby-in-Ashfield, Nottinghamshire

R. and J. Glencross, Over Haddon, Derbyshire

John O.K. Goode, Account Director, Snowdens Marquees

George Gosney, Dronfield Woodhouse, Derbyshire

Sheila and Michael Grimes, Haxby, Yorkshire

Mark and Lynne Hodgkinson

Anthony Knowelden, Sheffield

Patrick and Brooksbank, Ashbourne, Derbyshire

G.W. and S.M. Pattinson, Staffordshire

John A. Pickford, Endon, Staffordshire

Geoffrey O. Roberts, Bakewell, Derbyshire

Vicky Spender, Rowsley, Derbyshire

Mrs M. Stewart, High Peak, Derbyshire

Peter T. Sutherland, Walton Lodge, Chesterfield

Mrs Heather Swindell, Bakewell, Derbyshire

Philippa Tilbrook-Heath, Bakewell, Derbyshire

Judith M. Vale, Buxton, Derbyshire

Mr R. Walker, Alport, Nr Bakewell

John F.W. Walling, Newton Abbot, Devon

Mrs Gwen Watt, Bakewell, Derbyshire

Stuart N. Whittle, Market Warsop, Nottinghamshire

Jean and Brian Yates, Chesterfield, Derbyshire

Community Histories

The Book of Addiscombe • Canning and Clyde Road Residents Association and Friends
The Book of Addiscombe, Vol. II • Canning and Clyde Road Residents Association and Friends
The Book of Axminster with Kilmington • Les Berry and Gerald Gosling
The Book of Bampton • Caroline Seward
The Book of Barnstaple • Avril Stone
The Book of Barnstaple, Vol. II • Avril Stone
The Book of The Bedwyns • Bedwyn History Society
The Book of Bickington • Stuart Hands
Blandford Forum: A Millennium Portrait • Blandford Forum Town Council
The Book of Bramford • Bramford Local History Group
The Book of Breage & Germoe • Stephen Polglase
The Book of Bridestowe • D. Richard Cann
The Book of Bridport • Rodney Legg
The Book of Brixham • Frank Pearce
The Book of Buckfastleigh • Sandra Coleman
The Book of Buckland Monachorum & Yelverton • Pauline Hamilton-Leggett
The Book of Carharrack • Carharrack Old Cornwall Society
The Book of Carshalton • Stella Wilks and Gordon Rookledge
The Parish Book of Cerne Abbas • Vivian and Patricia Vale
The Book of Chagford • Iain Rice
The Book of Chapel-en-le-Frith • Mike Smith
The Book of Chittlehamholt with Warkleigh & Satterleigh • Richard Lethbridge
The Book of Chittlehampton • Various
The Book of Colney Heath • Bryan Lilley
The Book of Constantine • Moore and Trethowan
The Book of Cornwood and Lutton • Compiled by the People of the Parish
The Book of Creech St Michael • June Small
The Book of Cullompton • Compiled by the People of the Parish
The Book of Dawlish • Frank Pearce
The Book of Dulverton, Brushford, Bury & Exebridge • Dulverton and District Civic Society
The Book of Dunster • Hilary Binding
The Book of Edale • Gordon Miller
The Ellacombe Book • Sydney R. Langmead
The Book of Exmouth • W.H. Pascoe
The Book of Grampound with Creed • Bane and Oliver
The Book of Hayling Island & Langstone • Peter Rogers
The Book of Helston • Jenkin with Carter
The Book of Hemyock • Clist and Dracott
The Book of Herne Hill • Patricia Jenkyns
The Book of Hethersett • Hethersett Society Research Group
The Book of High Bickington • Avril Stone
The Book of Ilsington • Dick Wills
The Book of Kingskerswell • Carsewella Local History Group
The Book of Lamerton • Ann Cole and Friends
Lanner, A Cornish Mining Parish • Sharron Schwartz and Roger Parker
The Book of Leigh & Bransford • Malcolm Scott
The Book of Litcham with Lexham & Mileham • Litcham Historical and Amenity Society
The Book of Loddiswell • Loddiswell Parish History Group
The New Book of Lostwithiel • Barbara Fraser
The Book of Lulworth • Rodney Legg
The Book of Lustleigh • Joe Crowdy

The Book of Lyme Regis • Rodney Legg
The Book of Manaton • Compiled by the People of the Parish
The Book of Markyate • Markyate Local History Society
The Book of Mawnan • Mawnan Local History Group
The Book of Meavy • Pauline Hemery
The Book of Minehead with Alcombe • Binding and Stevens
The Book of Morchard Bishop • Jeff Kingaby
The Book of Newdigate • John Callcut
The Book of Nidderdale • Nidderdale Museum Society
The Book of Northlew with Ashbury • Northlew History Group
The Book of North Newton • J.C. and K.C. Robins
The Book of North Tawton • Baker, Hoare and Shields
The Book of Nynehead • Nynehead & District History Society
The Book of Okehampton • Roy and Ursula Radford
The Book of Paignton • Frank Pearce
The Book of Penge, Anerley & Crystal Palace • Peter Abbott
The Book of Peter Tavy with Cudlipptown • Peter Tavy Heritage Group
The Book of Pimperne • Jean Coull
The Book of Plymtree • Tony Eames
The Book of Porlock • Dennis Corner
Postbridge – The Heart of Dartmoor • Reg Bellamy
The Book of Priddy • Albert Thompson
The Book of Princetown • Dr Gardner-Thorpe
The Book of Rattery • By the People of the Parish
The Book of St Day • Joseph Mills and Paul Annear
The Book of Sampford Courtenay with Honeychurch • Stephanie Pouya
The Book of Sculthorpe • Gary Windeler
The Book of Seaton • Ted Gosling
The Book of Sidmouth • Ted Gosling and Sheila Luxton
The Book of Silverton • Silverton Local History Society
The Book of South Molton • Jonathan Edmunds
The Book of South Stoke with Midford • Edited by Robert Parfitt
South Tawton & South Zeal with Sticklepath • Roy and Ursula Radford
The Book of Sparkwell with Hemerdon & Lee Mill • Pam James
The Book of Staverton • Pete Lavis
The Book of Stithians • Stithians Parish History Group
The Book of Stogumber, Monksilver, Nettlecombe & Elworthy • Maurice and Joyce Chidgey
The Book of Studland • Rodney Legg
The Book of Swanage • Rodney Legg
The Book of Tavistock • Gerry Woodcock
The Book of Thorley • Sylvia McDonald and Bill Hardy
The Book of Torbay • Frank Pearce
The Book of Watchet • Compiled by David Banks
The Book of West Huntspill • By the People of the Parish
Widecombe-in-the-Moor • Stephen Woods
Widecombe – Uncle Tom Cobley & All • Stephen Woods
The Book of Williton • Michael Williams
The Book of Witheridge • Peter and Freda Tout and John Usmar
The Book of Withycombe • Chris Boyles
Woodbury: The Twentieth Century Revisited • Roger Stokes
The Book of Woolmer Green • Compiled by the People of the Parish

For details of any of the above titles or if you are interested in writing your own history, please contact:
Commissioning Editor, Community Histories, Halsgrove House, Lower Moor Way, Tiverton Business Park, Tiverton, Devon EX16 6SS, England;
email: naomic@halsgrove.com